The Over 60 Trivia Book

Bill Owen

St. Johann Press
Haworth, NJ

ST. JOHANN PRESS

Published in the United States of America
P.O. Box 241
Haworth, NJ 07641

Library of Congress Cataloging-in-Publication Data

Owen, Bill
    The over 60 trivia book / by Bill Owen.
        p. cm.
    ISBN 1-878282-21-2 (alk. paper)
    1. Questions and answers. I. title: Over sixty trivia book. II. Title.

AG195.O94 2001
031.02—dc21

                                  2001048315

The paper used in this publication meets the minimum requirements of American National Standard for Information Sciences—Permanence of Paper for Printed Library Materials, ANSI/NISO Z39.48-1992

Manufactured in the United States of America

Foreword

In the early 1950s I was a young staff announcer at NBC in Chicago. On Sunday mornings there was a lot of idle time between station breaks on the local station (WMAQ) and announcing a 9:00 A.M. organ program on the network. My friend Hugh Downs was at the beginning of his splendid career but was already well known enough to be on a somewhat loftier plateau, so he had plenty of Sabbath morning time on his hands. It happened that the well-known Windy City raconteur/author Studs Terkel did a weekend show, and it was his habit to drop into the announcers' lounge and chat it up with Hugh and me. One Sunday we fell to talking about early radio, and the next thing we knew we were quizzing each other. Who was Amos 'n' Andy's first announcer? What were Myrt and Marge's last names?

A few years later at WNEW in New York my first assignment was to emcee the all-night program, "The Milkman's Matinee." Only the loneliness of the sentinel of a graveyard from midnight to 6:00 A.M. remotely compares with the stark ennui of the overnight long-distance babbler on the radio. To refrain from going completely mad and starting to throw Frankie Laine and Patti Page records out the window onto Fifth Avenue, I started asking questions of my audience. As they say, if life hands you a lemon, squeeze it and start a soufflé. To my knowledge I was the first radio personality to use this sort of thing on the radio. Today they call it Trivia, and in time I came to be known as the King of same. Oh, well, I guess it's better than anonymity. On second thought, let me think about that.

In the years between then and now, of couse, Trivia has become a staple of broadcasting, both radio and television, and rare indeed is the station that doesn't have a record show host or sportscaster who doesn't use the device. Some are very good. Some merely have a open fact book in front of them. The kilocycles are full of poseurs.

That is why I took a somewhat jaundiced approach when advised that Mr. Bill Owen was a triviot nonpareil. Some bid so bold as to suggest that he could beat me at my own game with his tongue strapped behind him. The nerve! When we finally met, however, I was prepared to test him with a genuine Hall of Fame question. Facing the interloper with a studied coolness, I asked him, "Who, on her fatal flight, was Amelia Earhart's co-pilot?" with no hesitation and looking me right in the eye he replied, "Fred Noonan, of course." I think it was the coolness of the words "of course" that shook me. After asking him two additional questions of equal density and intensity, I proclaimed him the new King of Trivia and gave myself the modest honorific of Emperor of Esoterica. (I was tired anyway.)

Seriously, folks, Bill Owen is a hell of a guy. Over the years I have come to find out more about him. He was a child of the post-Depression and Second World War era, working first as a broadcaster in his native Midwest, doing everything from musical host (including some grand opera) to sports play-by-play to news and interviews. At one point in his career he was a cowboy on a children's show. In those days, like a berry picker, we went where the work was. He later moved to New York and joined the ABC televison and radio family. Not only did he handle sports but for ten years he was a regular substitute for Howard Cosell and lived to tell the story. Bill was also one of WABC Radio's original "Swinging Seven" DJs and later became the on-camera host of the Emmy-winning TV series for young people, "Discovery." During that period he also co-authored with Frank Buxton the books *Radio's Golden Age* and *The Big Broadcast 1920–1950*. These days he appears on radio and TV commercials and in his spare time lectures on old-time radio.

I'm certain that Bill joins me in insisting that Trivia is not trivial. It is far too important. And it is constantly replenishing itself. Today's fact is tomorrow's question. It just keeps rolling on.

Not unlike Bill Owen.

—Jim Lowe

[*Editor's note:* Jim Lowe, one of America's best-known DJs, is also a vocalist, pianist, and composer. The Springfield, MO, native had a number-one record in 1956 with his Dot label hit "The Green Door," which was on the charts for twenty-two weeks. Jim is still heard regularly on his nationally syndicated radio show "Jim Lowe and Friends."]

Preface

If you have had five dozen or more birthdays, as I have, perhaps you find yourself attracted to memories of those earlier times in your life and enjoy being reminded of World War II, Packards and Hudsons and Cords, Jack Benny and Edgar Bergen, Edward G. Robinson and Greer Garson, Mel Ott and Red Grange, The Dorsey Brothers and Benny Goodman. Especially when it comes to quiz programs and crossword puzzles and the like do I turn away from questions about rap performers, TV soap stars, Emmy winners, MTV, and computer lingo. If younger people get excited about such subjects, more power to them. But for me I'd rather recall those incredible motion pictures of the 1940s, oldtime radio (can you possibly compare Jimmy Durante, Eddie Cantor, Abbott and Costello, and Fibber McGee with the tasteless and cruel humor of some of the controversial late-night shows?) and all the other wonderful memories of those days that weren't necessarily better but seemed to have more substance. The material is arranged in question and answer form so you can make a game of it with friends or family. The difficulty of the questions varies from easy to almost impossible but achieving some sort of score is not the point. The fun is in seeing and hearing names and events that will take you back in time and trigger even more memories. I hope you have fun.

—Bill Owen

1. The principal "Axis" powers of World War II were, of course, Japan, Germany, and Italy. But there were six other nations that comprised the Axis. How many of them can you name?

2. Largely forgotten today is a once-common World War II term, "short-snorter." What was it?

3. Who was the first American given the title "General of the Armies of the United States"?

4. During World War II, four men were promoted to the rank of 5-star general. Can you name them?

5. A popular newspaper comic strip by Frank O. King that started in 1918 had its various characters age just as in real life. The main character came along three years later as a foundling left on Walt Wallet's doorstep. Can you name either the child or the strip?

6. Think carefully before you answer this. The answer is not as obvious as it would seem to be. If a person was born in 25 B.C. and died in A.D. 25, how many years did he live?

7. Babe Ruth was the highest paid baseball player in both the 1920s and 1930s. Who was highest paid in the 40s, 50s, and 60s?

8. Six well-known 20th century women had something in common. Knowing their *last* names would make it easy to identify their commonality. Can you figure it out from just their *first* names? Ida, Helen, Edith, Edith again, Florence, and Lou.

9. What would you guess is the most landed-upon space on a Monopoly board?

1. Hungary, Rumania, Bulgaria, Albania, Finland, and Thailand.

2. A short-snorter was a collection of bar tabs GI's amassed during the war. They would clip them together as evidence of the far-flung exotic places they had been to.

3. Surprisingly, not George Washington but John J. Pershing, who had the title conferred on him after World War I. It was not until 1976 that Washington was posthumously given that rank. In 1899, George Dewey was accorded a similar rank for the naval branch as "Admiral of the Navy."

4. George C. Marshall, Douglas MacArthur, Dwight D. Eisenhower, and Henry ("Hap") Arnold. At the same time the rank of Fleet Admiral was conferred on William D. Leahy, Ernest J. King, and Chester W. Nimitz. Later Omar Bradley got a fifth star and William F. ("Bull") Halsey was made Fleet Admiral.

5. Skeezix, which means both a mischievous child and a motherless calf, was the star of "Gasoline Alley." He eventually married his childhood sweetheart "Nina Clock."

6. The surprising answer: not 50 but 49 years. There was no year Zero, so 1 B.C. turned into A.D. 1 though, of course, those designations were not then in use.

7. Bob Feller in the 1940s, Ted Williams in the 50s, and Willie Mays in the 60s.

8. They were all First Ladies: Ida McKinley, Helen Taft, Edith Roosevelt, Edith Wilson, Florence Harding, and Lou Hoover.

9. Illinois. "Go" is second and B&O railroad third.

10. Here are the theme songs of four programs from Radio's Golden Age. See how many you can identify:

a. "Love in Bloom"
b. "The William Tell Overture"
c. "The Way You Look Tonight"
d. "One Hour With You"

11. Can you complete this radio jingle? "Don't despair, use your head, save your hair, use _____."

12. One nation literally switched continents in 1903 but not because of any natural disaster or land mass change. Can you guess what country it was?

13. The sobriquet "Bring 'em Back Alive" was applied to a famous adventurer of the 1930s and 40s. What was his name?

14. "Jimmie Lynch's "Death Dodgers" attracted huge crowds in the 1930s and 40s. What did they do?

15. The following men won fame during World War II in the same occupation, Gabriel Heatter, H. V. Kaltenborn, Quentin Reynolds, H. R. Baukhage, Cedric Foster, G.E.D., Boake Carter, and Raymond Gram Swing. What was their occupation?

16. One of the greatest college football players of all time earned the nickname "The Galloping Ghost." Who was he?

17. Rare is the person who can answer this correctly though it would seem to be quite easy. A hobo can make one cigar out of every five butts he finds. If he obtains 25 cigar butts, how many cigars can he make?

10.
- **a.** Jack Benny
- **b.** The Lone Ranger
- **c.** Mr. and Mrs. North
- **d.** Eddie Cantor

11. Fitch Shampoo

12. Panama. When it belonged to Colombia it was obviously part of South America. But on gaining its independence it became part of Central America which in turn is part of North America. Thus it moved from South America to North America.

13. Frank Buck.

14. Their specialty was defying death by smashing automobiles and jumping cars off a ramp over other cars as well as driving through fire. They often appeared at carnivals or state fairs.

15. They were all radio commentators.

16. Harold "Red" Grange of the University of Illinois.

17. Six cigars. Remember, after the hobo smokes five, he can make one more cigar from those five butts.

18. In 1933 Vincent Hamlin started a comic strip that was set in the kingdom of Moo in prehistoric times. Among the principal characters were Princess Oola, King Guzzle, a scientist named Dr. Wonmug, who had a Time Machine, and even a dinosaur named Dinny. What was the strip called?

19. Old-time radio had many famous pairs. For example, Fibber McGee and Molly. Try to complete these famous pairs from vintage radio:

a. Lum and _____
b. Myrt and _____
c. Billy and _____
d. Amos 'n' _____
e. Edgar Bergen and _____
f. Stoopnagle and _____
g. Vic and _____

20. Several big-band leaders of the 1930s and 40s had first names of only three letters. Can you supply the last name of the following? (In some cases there was more than one bandleader with the same first name.)

a. Les
b. Cab
c. Bob
d. Ina
e. Hal
f. Guy
g. Jan
h. Art
i. Abe
j. Ben

18. "Alley Oop."

19.
a. Lum and Abner
b. Myrt and Marge
c. Billy and Betty (a children's adventure program)
d. Amos 'n' Andy
e. Edgar Bergen and Charlie McCarthy
f. Stoopnagle and Budd
g. Vic and Sade

20.
a. Les Brown
b. Cab Calloway
c. Bob Crosby
d. Ina Ray Hutton
e. Hal Kemp (or Hal McIntire)
f. Guy Lombardo
g. Jan Garber (or Jan Savitt)
h. Art Kassel (or Art Mooney)
i. Abe Lyman
j. Ben Bernie (or Ben Pollack or Ben Selvin)

"The Shadow"

21. There have been many famous fictional dogs. Try to name the canine character associated with the following:

a. Little Orphan Annie
b. Blondie and Dagwood
c. Little Annie Rooney
d. Buster Brown
e. The Thin Man Nick Charles
f. Dennis the Menace
g. The dog in the Our Gang Comedies

22. Remember the great radio commercials of a time gone by? "Duz does Everything." "Pepsi-Cola hits the spot." "J-E-L-L-O." All were colorful commercials. Others were so colorful they contained the name of a color in their slogan. See if you can identify the color associated with the following commercials:

a. "Lucky Strike_____ has gone to war."
b. "You'll wonder where the_____ went when you brush your teeth with Pepsodent."
c. "99 and 44/100% pure. It floats."
d. "Rinso _____, Rinso _____, happy little washday song."
e. _____Coal.

23. In the 1940s there were three actresses named McDonald or MacDonald. Two of them sang as well as acted. How many of the three McDonalds can you think of?

24. Ike was a familiar nickname during World War II as Dwight Eisenhower rose to prominence. There was *Slam* Marshall and the unforgettable *Monty*, the nickname for British field marshal Bernard Montgomery. See if you can recall the last names of these World War II figures:

a. Vinegar Joe
b. The Desert Fox
c. Howlin' Mad
d. Bull
e. Hap

21.
a. Sandy
b. Daisy (or her pup Elmer)
c. Zero
d. Tige
e. Asta
f. Ruff
g. Pete the pup

22.
a. Green
b. Yellow
c. Ivory
d. White
e. Blue

23. Jeanette MacDonald, who appeared on screen often with Nelson Eddy. Another singer named Grace McDonald and a beautiful actress whose nickname was The Body—Marie McDonald.

24.
a. Vinegar Joe Stilwell, our outspoken general in Burma
b. German field marshal Erwin Rommel
c. Marine Corps general Holland Smith who led his troops in Saipan, Tarawa, and Iwo Jima
d. The aggressive U.S. Admiral William F. Halsey
e. Henry H. Arnold, chief of the Army Air Forces

25. There have been many people named Nelson in show business. Barry Nelson the actor and Willie Nelson the country singer to name a couple. It's a common name *outside* of show business too: Donald Nelson the head of the War Production Board under FDR during World War II and of course Nelson Mandela, the South African leader. See if you can identify the following people named Nelson:

a. A prominent bandleader in the early days of radio who later had a popular TV show featuring his wife and two sons
b. A well-known dancer in movies of the 1940s and 50s
c. A notorious gangster known by a nickname in place of his first name
d. A highly respected storyteller on radio who often played all the parts in his tales. His *first* name was Nelson

26. Here are the first names of some singing sisters. Try to come up with their last name.

a. Patty, Maxene, and LaVerne
b. Rosemary and Betty
c. Connee, Martha, and Vet (Helvetia)
d. Christine, Dorothy, and Phyllis
e. Marge, Bea, and Geri
f. Ginger, Lou, and Jean

27. The Brooklyn Dodgers played the New York Yankees in seven different World Series. Amazingly, one Brooklyn player appeared in every inning of every game in all those series. Who was he?

28. Here are the names of some characters from old-time comic strips. See if you can name the strip.

a. Dale Arden
b. Corky
c. Herby
d. Rollo

25.
a. Ozzie Nelson
b. Gene Nelson
c. Babyface Nelson
d. Nelson Olmsted

26.
a. Patty, Maxene, and LaVerne Andrews
b. Rosemary and Betty Clooney
c. Connee, Martha, and Vet Boswell (Connee continued as a big band soloist after being afflicted with polio and confined to a wheel chair.)
d. Christine, Dorothy, and Phyllis McGuire
e. Ginger, Lou, and Jean Dinning

27. PeeWee Reese, the great Dodger shortstop. The seven series covered a span from 1941–1956.

28.
a. "Flash Gordon." Dale was Flash's girl friend.
b. "Gasoline Alley." He was the brother of Skeezix.
c. "Smitty." Herby was the baby brother of office boy Smitty.
d. "The Katzenjammer Kids." Rollo was the nemesis of Hans and Fritz, always trying to get them into trouble in order to impress his girl friend Lena.

The Lone Ranger and Silver

29. America's First Ladies have a secure place in history from Martha Washington to the present. Women such as Dolley Madison, Mary Lincoln, Eleanor Roosevelt, and Mamie Eisenhower. But how many wives can you name of *losing* presidential candidates? Try to remember the first name of the wives of the following losing candidates:

a. Dukakis
b. Humphrey
c. Goldwater
d. Willkie
e. Dewey

30. Certain vintage radio programs are associated with a particular sponsor: "The Shadow" and Blue Coal.... "Take It Or Leave It, The 64 Dollar Question" with Eversharp...and "Edgar Bergen and Charlie McCarthy" with Chase and Sanborn coffee. See if you can name the loyal sponsor that presented the following programs for many years.

a. "Little Orphan Annie"
b. "Dr. I.Q."
c. "Mr. District Attorney"
d. "Dr. Christian"

31. Jackie Robinson broke modern big league baseball's racial barrier in 1947. But what player was *second?*

32. In the era of motion picture serials, also known as chapterplays, one studio produced far more than any other. Which studio was it?

29.
a. Kitty
b. Muriel
c. Peggy
d. Edith
e. Frances

30.
a. Ovaltine
b. Mars candy
c. Bristol-Myers advertising Ipana for the Smile of Beauty and Sal Hepatica for the Smile of Health.
d. Vaseline

31. Larry Doby with Cleveland also in 1947

32. Republic Pictures

Tom Mix with Tony,
the Wonder Horse

33. Let's recall four famous songs you've heard many times. Try to name the song from the following clues:

a. In what song do the deer and the antelope play?
b. What song claims "He doesn't know a rumba from a waltz"?
c. What song mentions Granada and Asbury Park and "good turtle soup or merely the mock"?
d. What song mentions Edison, Marconi, Fulton, Whitney, Milton Hershey, the Wright brothers, Henry Ford, and Columbus?

34. We have come across many cheerful-sounding names over the years. See if you can identify the following people:

a. A Western sidekick whose first name was Smiley
b. A comic strip character whose first name was Happy
c. A notorious criminal named Laffy Smith appeared in a well-known comic strip in 1943... what was the strip?
d. On what radio comedy program was Kitty O'Neil, the Laughing Lady, a regular?
e. Finally, who was billed as "The singer with a smile in his voice"?

35. Here are nicknames of some famous people from the past. Try to identify each one.

a. The Doaker
b. The Clown Prince of Baseball
c. The Sage of Winston County, Alabama
d. The Old Curmudgeon

36. Grace Kelly began her film career in 1951 in a movie called *Fourteen Hours*. Emmett Kelly was renowned as a circus clown. Jack Kelly starred on television as Bart Maverick. There were also four famous Kellys who starred in movies in the 1940s. How many can you think of?

33.
a. "Home on the Range," the official state song of Kansas
b. "The Gentleman Is a Dope"
c. "At Long Last Love"
d. "They All Laughed," written by George and Ira Gershwin in 1937

34.
a. Smiley Burnette
b. Happy Hooligan
c. Dick Tracy
d. Al Pearce and His Gang
e. Jack Smith

35.
a. Doak Walker, the versatile halfback from SMU, winner of the 1948 Heisman Trophy
b. Al Schacht, who had been a major league pitcher with Washington for three seasons before becoming a baseball clown...he wound up with a 14–10 career pitching record
c. Pat Buttram, a regular on radio's National Barn Dance. He played comic characters in the movies and eventually re-placed Smiley Burnette as Gene Autry's sidekick
d. Harold Ickes, an FDR intimate and Secretary of the Interior

36.
Gene Kelly, the dancer
Nancy Kelly, who won an Oscar nomination for her role in *The Bad Seed*
Wisecracking Patsy Kelly, who often played a maid
Paul Kelly, a leading man in B pictures.

37. Every big band in the 1930s and 40s had a theme song. Name the bandleaders who used the following:

a. "Auld Lang Syne"
b. "Moonlight Serenade"
c. "Bubbles in the Wine"
d. "Ciribiribin"
e. "I'm Getting Sentimental Over You"
f. "My Shawl"

38. What celebrities answered to these nicknames?

a. Hollywood's King
b. The King of the Cowboys
c. The Wild Hoss of the Osage
d. America's Sweetheart
e. America's Boy Friend

39. There are two words in the English language that contain the first 6 letters of the alphabet yet are only 8 letters long each. What are the two words?

40. Only three common words in English begin with the letters DW. How many of the three can you think of?

41. Here are more celebrity nicknames. Try to identify each of them.

a. The Great Profile
b. Der Bingle
c. Master Melvin
d. Cactus Jack
e. The Old Maestro
f. The Flying Finn

37.
a. Guy Lombardo
b. Glenn Miller
c. Lawrence Welk
d. Harry James
e. Tommy Dorsey
f. Xavier Cugat

38.
a. Clark Gable
b. Roy Rogers
c. Baseball player Pepper Martin
d. Mary Pickford
e. Buddy Rogers

39. Boldface and Feedback

40. Dwarf Dwell Dwindle

41.
a. John Barrymore
b. Bing Crosby
c. Mel Ott
d. U.S. Vice President John Garner
e. Bandleader Ben Bernie
f. Finnish distance runner Paavo Nurmi

42. Let's try to recall the wives of old-time radio.

a. Who was Mary Livingstone married to?
b. How about Portland Hoffa?
c. Tootsie Woodley
d. Nora Charles
e. Fanny Barbour

43. Here is a list of states. Try to figure out logically which state would come next in the list: Vermont, Connecticut, Virginia, Tennessee, New York, Kentucky, Indiana, _____?

44. Here are the theme songs of some famous radio programs. Try to name the show that used each one:

a. "The Perfect Song"
b. "Smile, Darn Ya, Smile"
c. "The Red River Valley"
d. "The March from The Love for Three Oranges"

45. Here are the last names of some famous comedy teams of the past. Try to recall their first names.

a. Nelson and Hilliard
b. Elliott and Goulding
c. Jones and Brown
d. Edwards and Peabody

46. Here are some fictional characters we used to hear on vintage radio. Try to recall their *first* names.

a. Gildersleeve
b. Riley from "The Life of Riley"
c. Dr. Watson, Sherlock Holmes' assistant
d. Colonel Stoopnagle of Stoopnagle and Budd comedy team

42.
a. Jack Benny
b. Fred Allen
c. Herb Woodley, the neighbor of Dagwood and Blondie Bumstead
d. Nick Charles, the Thin Man
e. Henry Barbour, the patriarch of "One Man's Family"

43. Illinois. These are state names used in properties in the game Monopoly as you advance around the board. The last ones would be North Carolina and Pennsylvania.

44.
a. "Amos 'n' Andy"
b. "Fred Allen Show"
c. "Our Gal Sunday"
d. "The FBI in Peace and War"

45.
a. Ozzie and Harriet
b. Bob and Ray
c. Amos 'n' Andy, played by Freeman Gosden and Charles Correll
d. Lum and Abner, played by Chester Lauck and Norris Goff

46.
a. Throckmorton P. Gildersleeve
b. Chester A. Riley
c. Dr. John Watson
d. Colonel Lemuel Q. Stoopnagle

47. There is only one number that when spelled out has all its letters in alphabetical order. Can you identify the number?

48. There have been many famous sisters in show business. The Andrews sisters, the McGuire sisters and so on. Try to identify the following sisters from just their first names:

a. Joan and Olivia
b. Constance, Joan, and Barbara
c. Natalie, Norma, and Constance
d. Jane, Helen, and Patti

49. Here are some commercials from the Golden Age of radio. Try to identify each sponsor:

a. So round, so firm, so fully-packed, so free and easy on the draw.
b. No brush, no lather, no rub-in. Wet your razor, then begin.
c. For a picture of Buck Rogers, just send in two inches of the strip of tin that comes off the can when you open it.
d. The breakfast cereal shot from guns!

50. In the 1940s only three major Hollywood male stars had a last name beginning with the letter V. Who were they?

51. When you list our fifty states alphabetically, in only two cases are states next to each other in the list also neighbors on the *map*. Can you think of those two pairs of states?

52. Many actors have been associated with one particular role. Try to recall the roles associated with the following actors:

a. Basil Rathbone
b. Lew Ayres
c. Warner Oland
d. Chester Morris
e. Leo Gorcey
f. Roland Young

47. Forty

48.
a. Joan Fontaine and Olivia De Havilland
b. Constance, Joan, and Barbara Bennett (Barbara, the oldest, was in some silent films while Joan, the youngest of the three, and Constance were both major stars of the 30s, 40s, and beyond)
c. Natalie, Norma, and Constance Talmadge (Norma was the oldest and a silent screen heroine, Constance was a silent heroine and comedienne, and Natalie, the youngest, made a few silent comedies and then retired to marry Buster Keaton)
d. Jane, Helen, and Patti Pickens. The Pickens Sisters were a popular vocal trio in the 1930s

49.
a. Lucky Strike Cigarettes
b. Barbasol
c. Cocomalt
d. Quaker Puffed Wheat and Quaker Puffed Rice

50.
Rudy Vallee, Conrad Veidt, and Erich Von Stroheim

51. Illinois and Indiana   Florida and Georgia

52.
a. Sherlock Holmes
b. Dr. Kildare
c. Charlie Chan
d. Boston Blackie
e. Slip Mahoney of the Bowery Boys
f. Topper

53. Here is a list of 5 famous men. Each of them had an equally famous son-in-law. See how many you can name.

a. Cecil B. De Mille
b. Franz Liszt
c. Eugene O'Neill
d. Tom Harmon
e. Arturo Toscanini

54. The final score of the most famous baseball game ever played was 4–2. Who was playing?

55. See if you can supply the last name of the following people:

a. Slapsie Maxie
b. Man Mountain
c. Brick (a fictional hero)
d. Machine Gun

56. J-A-N is an unusual combination of letters to start a word. Except for the month of January and people's names such as Jane and Janet only two common words in English begin with J-A-N. Can you think of both of them?

57. Many glamorous names of now extinct automobiles haunt our memories, names like Packard, Cord, DeSoto, LaSalle. There were also some automobile companies with *two-word* names. Try to recall the second half of the following carmakers:

a. Pierce-
b. Graham-
c. Kaiser-
d. Willys-

53.
a. Anthony Quinn
b. Richard Wagner (who was only a year-and-a-half younger than his father-in-law Liszt)
c. Charlie Chaplin (who was only six months younger than his father-in-law O'Neill)
d. Ricky Nelson
e. Vladimir Horowitz

54.
Mudville lost to an unidentified team in the poem "Casey at the Bat"

55.
a. Slapsie Maxie Rosenbloom was a boxer turned movie actor. His first film was *Mr. Broadway* in 1933.
b. Man Mountain Dean, a wrestler who played comedy parts in films of the 1930s
c. Brick Bradford, a space hero who first appeared in August of 1933, more than four years after the debut of Buck Rogers but some five months before Flash Gordon.
d. Machine Gun Kelly, a notorious outlaw whose real first name was George. He was a kidnapper and bootlegger but he never fired his machine gun in the commission of a crime.

56. Jangle and Janitor

57.
a. Pierce-Arrow
b. Graham-Paige, built by brothers Joseph, Robert, and Ray Graham who bought the old Paige Motor Company in 1927.
c. Kaiser-Frazer, a merger of carmakers Henry J. Kaiser and Joseph W. Frazer. Kaiser gained fame as a rapid builder of liberty ships during World War II.
d. Willys-Overland, a company that was formed when John Willys, an Elmira, New York car dealer bought the ailing Overland firm of Indianapolis

58. *E* is the most commonly used letter in the English language. Which is the *least* used?

59. A number of famous football players are known by their nickname. Try to identify the following gridiron stars:

a. The Gipper
b. Night Train
c. Crazy Legs
d. Mr. Outside
e. Spec

60. Many fictional heroes have had able assistants at their side. Try to identify the fictional hero each of the following assisted:

a. Tonto
b. Dr. Watson
c. Margot Lane
d. Kato
e. Paul Drake
f. Runt

61. There are 6 ordinary words in the English language that are 6 letters long and contain all their letters in alphabetical order. See if you can think of one of them.

62. Here are the names of some once familiar characters from comic strips. Try to name the strip in which each appeared.

a. Available Jones
b. Fatstuff
c. Knobby Walsh
d. Lord Plushbottom

58. *Z* as in zebra, *X* is runner-up, followed by *Q*.

59.
a. George Gipp of Notre Dame
b. Dick "Night Train" Lane, who was married for a time to singer Dinah Washington
c. Elroy Hirsch, a Big Ten star who later played for the Los Angeles Rams.
d. Glenn Davis, half of Army's legendary Mr. Inside and Mr. Outside combination. Mr. Inside was Doc Blanchard who ran up the middle while Davis headed around end.
e. Orban "Spec" Sanders, who twice led the old All-America football Conference in rushing while playing with the New York Yankees. (That's correct: the New York Yankees *football* team.)

60.
a. The Lone Ranger
b. Sherlock Holmes
c. The Shadow
d. The Green Hornet
e. Perry Mason
f. Boston Blackie

61. Abhors   Almost   Begins   Biopsy   Chintz   Chimps

62.
a. "Li'l Abner"
b. "Smilin' Jack" (Fatstuff was the South Sea island native who was forever popping shirt buttons caught by a chicken)
c. "Joe Palooka" (Knobby was his fight manager)
d. "Moon Mullins"

63. Many fictional heroes are better known by a second identity. For instance, Clark Kent is better known as Superman. Try to name the better-known identity of the following:

a. Lamont Cranston
b. Billy Batson
c. John Reid
d. Brad Runyon
e. Michael Lanyard

64. Here are some names you may or may not find familiar. What do they have in common? Earl Derr Biggers, Leslie Charteris, Rex Stout, and Raymond Chandler

65. There have been many romantic teams in the movies. Janet Gaynor and Charles Farrell made eleven appearances together on screen. Dick Powell and Joan Blondell made ten, as did Fred Astaire and Ginger Rogers. Other romantic teams that come to mind are Spencer Tracy and Katharine Hepburn, Richard Burton and Elizabeth Taylor, Judy Garland and Mickey Rooney, and Nelson Eddy and Jeanette MacDonald. But one actor and actress appeared together a record *twelve* times. Can you name them?

66. There is something very special about this number: 8,549,176,320. Yes, it does contain all ten single digits, but that's not the answer. Why is it unique?

67. Now here is a question you have to ask someone else. The words are spelled correctly here. This is the world's most difficult spelling test. Ask someone to spell the words in these four common phrases:

a. rack one's brains
b. just deserts
c. dire straits
d. rite of passage

63.
a. The Shadow
b. Captain Marvel
c. The Lone Ranger
d. The Fat Man
e. The Lone Wolf, a reformed jewel thief who later became a detective

64. They all created fictional detectives. Earl Derr Biggers (Charlie Chan), Leslie Charteris (The Saint), Rex Stout (Nero Wolfe), and Raymond Chandler (The Adventures of Philip Marlowe)

65. William Powell and Myrna Loy appeared six times together in the Thin Man series and twelve times altogether as a romantic team.

66. When spelled out, the numbers are in alphabetical order.

67.
a. Rack is spelled r-a-c-k in this phrase.
b. Deserts is d-e-s-e-r-t-s because it refers to what one *deserves* and has nothing to do with food.
c. Straits is spelled s-t-r-a-i-t-s since it refers to a narrow passageway as in The Straits of Magellan.
d. Rite is spelled r-i-t-e since it refers to a ritual, not to something one is entitled to.

68. We're going back to vintage radio now. Try to identify the program on which we heard each of the following:

a. I know many things, for I walk by night. I know many strange tales hidden in the hearts of men and women who have stepped into the shadows.
b. On what program did we hear "Holy Mackerel" and "Now ain't dat sumpin'"?
c. Champion of the people. Defender of truth. Guardian of our fundamental rights to life, liberty, and the pursuit of happiness.

69. Let's return to the Hollywood films of the 1940s. See if you can think of five stars of that era whose last name was Young.

70. Again, let's return to the Golden Age of Hollywood movies. There were nine major studios that turned out films in those days. Five of them were known as the Big Five; two were called the Little Two. There were two other studios that were also active in producing films. How many of those nine studios can you name?

68.
a. "The Whistler"
b. "Amos 'n' Andy"
c. "Mr. District Attorney"

69. Loretta Young, whose career in films began accidentally at age 15 when she answered a studio call meant for her older sister Polly Ann Young.

Robert Young, who later starred on television on "Father Knows Best" and as "Marcus Welby, M.D."

Gig Young who was a star in the 40s, 50s, 60s, and 70s. He won an Academy Award in 1969 for his role in the dance marathon movie *They Shoot Horses, Don't They?* Elizabeth Montgomery was one of his five real-life wives.

Roland Young, best known for the title role in the Topper series.

Alan Young, the comic actor who debuted in *Margie* in 1946 and appeared in such later films as *Mr. Belvedere Goes to College, Aaron Slick from Punkin Crick,* and *Androcles and the Lion.* Give yourself extra credit if you came up with a 6th...Victor Sen-Young, who spelled his name Y-U-N-G. He had a long run as Charlie Chan's Number One Son. Keye Luke, by the way was Number Two Son.

70. The Big Five were MGM (the biggest of them all), Warner Brothers, 20th Century Fox, Paramount, and RKO. The so-called Little Two were Columbia and Universal. The other two were Republic, the king of movie serials, and Allied Artists, whose best-known subsidiary was Monogram Pictures that churned out many films of Charlie Chan and The Bowery Boys. Allied Artists produced such quality movies as *Love in the Afternoon* and *Friendly Persuasion.* United Artists was not a studio but basically a distribution company founded by Mary Pickford, Douglas Fairbanks, Sr., Charlie Chaplin, and D. W. Griffith.

71. We're going back to the wonderful world of the comic strips of a bygone era to try to recall the name of the strip in which the following characters appeared:

a. Tilda, the maid
b. Lillums, the girl friend of the star of the strip
c. Downwind Jaxon
d. Utah

72. Let's go back to those remarkable days of radio's Golden Age. See if you can identify the programs on which we heard the following openings:

a. Return with us now to those thrilling days of yesteryear.
b. And now here is that wise man with the friendly smile and the cash for your correct answers...
c. The story asks the question ... can this girl from a mining town in the West find happiness as the wife of a wealthy and titled Englishman?
d. Who knows what evil lurks in the hearts of men?

73. See if you can identify five famous big bands from their band or bandleader's slogan.

a. The King of Swing
b. The Sweetest Music This Side of Heaven
c. The Band of Renown
d. Rippling Rhythm
e. The Idol of the Air Lanes

74. Let's recall some of the great comedy teams of show business from only the first initial of the comedians. For example, A&C would be Abbott and Costello.

a. L&H
b. B&A
c. W&W
d. FM&M
e. O&J

71.

a. "The Gumps"

b. "Harold Teen"

c. "Smilin' Jack" (Downwind was always drawn only in profile and readers were tantalized hoping one day to see his face)

d. "Little Joe," a strip set in the cowboy era West.

72.

a. "The Lone Ranger"

b. "Dr. I.Q."

c. "Our Gal Sunday"

d. "The Shadow"

73.

a. Benny Goodman

b. Guy Lombardo and His Royal Canadians

c. Les Brown

d. Shep Fields, the famous sound effect was made simply by blowing a drinking straw into a glass of water

e. Jan Garber

74.

a. Laurel and Hardy

b. Burns and Allen

c. Wheeler and Woolsey, who were featured in many zany films of the 1930s

d. Fibber McGee and Molly, played by real-life married couple Jim and Marian Jordan

e. Olsen and Johnson, best remembered for their antics in the show and movie *Hellzapoppin*

75. Many brothers have attained fame in the same field. Try to identify the following brothers from only their first names:

a. Joe, Dominic, and Vince
b. Julius, Arthur, Leonard, and Herbert
c. Ham and Bud
d. Dana and Steve

76. Here are some groups of names, some of which may be familiar while others may not. See if you can figure out what each group had in common.

a. Jerry Siegel and Joe Shuster, Bob Kane, Ed Herren, Johnston McCulley
b. Harold Gray, Milton Caniff, Chester Gould, Al Capp
c. Dashiell Hammett, Rex Stout, Lesile Charteris, and the team of Frederic Dannay and Manfred Bennington Lee

77. Many comedians had colorful names such as Groucho. In fact, there were nine male comedians whose first or last name is itself the name of a color. How many can you think of?

78. Many of us still remember the commercials we heard during radio's Golden Age. The most famous jingle of all was "Pepsi-Cola hits the spot, 12 full ounces, that's a lot. Twice as much for a nickel too...Pepsi-Cola is the drink for you." That first appeared on radio in 1939. See if you can identify the sponsor of the following:

a. Avoid 5 o'clock shadow!
b. The pen that's guaranteed not for years, not for life, but guaranteed *forever!*
c. Rich, rich, rich with flavor. Smooth, smooth, smooth as silk. More food energy than sweet, fresh milk!
d. Push, pull. Click, click. Change blades that quick.

75.
a. Joe, Dominic, and Vince DiMaggio
b. The Marx Brothers, Groucho, Harpo, Chico, and Zeppo
c. Ham and Bud Fisher (Ham drew "Joe Palooka" of the comic strips while Bud did "Mutt and Jeff")
d. Dana Andrews and Steve Forrest (Dana's real name was Carver Daniel Andrews, his brother's was William Forrest Andrews)

76.
a. They all created caped heroes...Superman, Batman, Captain Marvel and Zorro (Zorro means fox in Spanish)
b. They created famous comic strips..."Little Orphan Annie," "Terry and the Pirates" as well as "Steve Canyon," "Dick Tracy," and "Li'l Abner"
c. They created fictional detectives... Sam Spade as well as The Thin Man and The Fat Man, Nero Wolfe, The Saint, and Ellery Queen

77. Shecky Greene, Joe E. Brown, Redd Foxx, Red Skelton, Red Buttons, Slammy White, Pinky Lee, Phil Silvers, and Ben Blue

78.
a. Gem Blades
b. Eversharp pens
c. Royal Pudding
d. Schick injector razor

79. When you see the initials MM you perhaps think right away of Marilyn Monroe. She did indeed make those initials famous. But there were many other celebrities with the same initials—MM. Try to identify them from these clues:

a. A character actress of movies of the 1930s, 40s and 50s best remembered as Ma Kettle
b. A shortstop for the St. Louis Cardinals, known as "The Octopus"
c. A musical comedy star and the mother of a famous TV star
d. A superhero of Terrytoons cartoons beginning in 1942

80. Thirteen nations of the world were named for people. We'll tell you the five most obscure ones and you try to identify the other eight. San Marino is named for St. Marinus. Sao Tomé and Principe for St. Thomas. St. Lucia is named for St. Lucy. St. Kitts and Nevis for Christopher Columbus (Kitt is short for Christopher). St.Vincent and The Grenadines for a Spanish priest St. Vincent. Now try to name the other eight nations named for people.

81. Aside from any type of diving or acrobatics, there are three sports that are won by going backwards. Can you name all three?

82. Many of us remember moments from the old radio shows of the Golden Age. Try to recall on which program we heard the following:

a. A shy door-to-door salesman knocking on a door and then muttering to himself "Nobody's home, I hope, I hope, I hope!"
b. The double click of a camera shutter followed by the star of the show exclaiming, "Got it! Look for it in *The Morning Express!*"
c. "Great trains dive with a roar into the two-and-one-half-mile tunnel which burrows beneath the glitter and swank of Park Avenue. And then..."
d. "The story of a woman who sets out to prove what so many other women long to prove in their own lives. That romance can live on at 35 ... and even beyond."

79.
a. Marjorie Main
b. Marty Marion
c. Mary Martin, mother of Larry Hagman
d. Mighty Mouse

80.
Bolivia, named for Simon Bolivar
China for Emperor Chin
Colombia for Christopher Columbus
El Salvador for "The Savior" (Christ)
The Philippines for King Philip II
Saudi Arabia for King Saud
The Solomon Islands for King Solomon
The United States of America for Amerigo Vespucci

81. rowing, swimming the backstroke, tug-of-war

82.
a. Al Pearce as Elmer Blurt on "Al Pearce and His Gang"
b. "Casey, Crime Photographer"
c. "Grand Central Station" ("Crossroads of a million private lives.")
d. "The Romance of Helen Trent"

83. Many popular singers have had memorable nicknames. Try to identify the following:

a. The Groaner
b. The Cruising Crooner
c. The Park Avenue Hillbilly
d. The Louisiana Lark

84. Many celebrities have the same name as months of the year: singer *April* Stevens, actress *Mae* West (though she spelled it differently from the month) and *June* Christy. But there are also some famous names that are the same as days of the week. See if you can identify the celebrities by these brief descriptions:

a. A famous baseball player of the 19th century who became even more famous as a preacher. His last name is a day of the week.
b. An actress married to Dudley Moore. She was nominated for an Academy Award for *Looking for Mr. Goodbar*. Her first name is a day of the week.
c. Another baseball player, an outfielder who started out with Kansas City in 1966 before moving over to Oakland. His last name is a day of the week.
d. A fictional detective sergeant for the LAPD, played by Jack Webb. His last name is a day of the week.

85. Here's a puzzle that requires some clear thinking: If three days ago was the day before Friday, what will the day after tomorrow be?

83.
a. Bing Crosby
b. Jack Owens on "The Breakfast Club"
c. Dorothy Shay, who was featured on the "Spike Jones Show" on radio
d. Jack Baker, another singer on "Don MacNeill's Breakfast Club"

84.
a. Billy Sunday
b. Tuesday Weld
c. Rick Monday
d. Joe Friday

85. Tuesday (Thursday being three days ago means it's now Sunday so the day after tomorrow would be Tuesday)

The Andrews Sisters (l-r) Maxene, Patty, and La Verne

86. Back in the days of vintage radio, we came across many doctors as we twisted the dial. See if you can identify the doctors from these descriptions:

a. A doctor who asked questions and gave away silver dollars for correct answers.
b. A doctor played by Jean Hersholt on a program on which the listening audience was invited to write the scripts with a payment of two thousand dollars for the best script of the year.
c. A doctor who constantly sparred verbally with Fibber McGee who would call him an "epidemic chaser" or perhaps "a sap-headed serum salesman."
d. A former criminal who became a psychiatrist specializing in keeping ex-cons out of trouble while he aided the police in solving crimes.

87. Historians tell us that Hitler was a piker when it came to conquering territory, at least compared with other aggressors from history. Adolf is only sixth on the all-time list. See if you can figure out the five who ranked ahead of him.

88. Here are a couple more nicknames of celebrities from a bygone era. Can you name them both?

a. The Kingfish
b. The Poor Little Rich Girl

89. In a standard deck of cards, only one King does not have a mustache. Which one?

86.
a. Dr. I.Q.
b. Dr. Christian
c. Doc Gamble
d. Crime Doctor

87. Ranking fifth, just ahead of Hitler, is Attila the Hun. Number four is Cyrus the great. Third is Tamerlane. Number two is Alexander the Great. And atop the conqueror list is the dreaded Genghis Khan. (In case you're interested in the rest of the top ten, Napoleon ranks seventh, Mahmud of Ghanzi (Near Eastern Empire) is eighth, number nine is Pizarro, with Cortcs number ten.

88.
a. Political leader Huey Long
b. Barbara Hutton, the often unhappy heiress to the Woolworth fortune

89. The King of Hearts

Orson Welles

90. Back in the days of old-time radio, many forms of transportation were featured on various programs such as The Lone Ranger's horse Silver and Buck Rogers' spaceship. On what programs were the following featured:

a. The Black Beauty automobile
b. Tony the Wonder Horse
c. A Maxwell automobile
d. The Silver Albatross, an amphibian airplane

91. In the 1920s, a sophisticated group of men and women met regularly in the Rose Room of New York's Algonquin Hotel. How many of the nine basic members known as the Algonquin Wits can you remember? (Two were women, both writers)

92. Here are some excerpts from the openings of famous radio shows from the Golden Age. Try to identify the programs from these snippets:

a. Anyone can send in a joke and if your joke is told by our storytelling genius Peter Donald you get ten dollars.
b. Uh-uh-uh. Don't touch that dial. It's time for....
c. The best-sellers in sheet music and phonograph records, the songs most heard on the air and most played in the automatic coin machines...an accurate, authentic tabulation of America's taste in popular music.
d. Out of the fog, out of the night...and into his American adventures comes...

90.

a. "The Green Hornet"

b. "Tom Mix"

c. "Jack Benny," with the sound provided by Mel Blanc

d. "Jack Armstrong, the All-American Boy"

91.

Dorothy Parker, writer

Edna Ferber, writer

George S. Kaufman, playwright

Robert Sherwood, playwright

Franklin P. Adams, author of a newspaper column called "The Conning Tower"

Heywood Broun, author of a newspaper column titled "It Seems To Me"

Ring Lardner, writer

Robert Benchley, writer and humorist

Alexander Woollcott, writer

There were others who joined them from time to time, such as Noel Coward, Alfred Lunt and Lynn Fontanne, Harpo Marx, Paul Robeson, Charles MacArthur, Harold Ross of the *New Yorker* magazine, and Tallulah Bankhead.

92.

a. "Can You Top This?"

b. "Blondie"

c. "Your Hit Parade"

d. "Bulldog Drummond"

93. Guy Fawkes made his mark in history and Guy de Maupassant in literature. See if you can name three *entertainers* with the first name of Guy.

a. One was a bald-headed character actor seen in such films as *Babbitt, Mr. Smith Goes to Washington,* and *Scattergood Baines*
b. Another was a leading man in films who won his greatest fame portraying a Western hero on television in the 1950s.
c. The third was a popular singer with such hits as "My Heart Cries for You" and "Sparrow in the Treetop."

94. During radio's Golden Age, the success of programs often depended on the cast of supporting characters. Jack Benny was aided by Mary Livingstone, Dennis Day, Phil Harris, and Mel Blanc. Try to name the program that featured the following characters:

a. Senator Claghorn, Mrs. Nussbaum, Titus Moody, and Ajax Cassidy
b. Kingfish, Madame Queen, Shorty the barber, and Stonewall the lawyer
c. Phillip Boynton, Osgood Conklin, Stretch Snodgrass, and Mrs. Davis the landlady
d. Grandpappy Spears, Dick Huddleston the postmaster, Snake Hogan, and Squire Skimp

95. Here's an interesting challenge. Try to figure out which pair does *not* belong in this list of five word pairs: Mike and Victor, Romeo and Juliet, Quebec and Lima, Rum and Brandy, and Tango and Foxtrot

93.
a. Guy Kibbee
b. Guy Madison (he played Wild Bill Hickok on TV)
c. Guy Mitchell

94.
a. "Fred Allen"
b. "Amos 'n' Andy"
c. "Our Miss Brooks" (starring Eve Arden)
d. "Lum and Abner"

95. Rum and Brandy does not belong on the list. All the others are part of the international Phonetic Alphabet which now begins with Alpha, Bravo, Charlie. During World War II it began Able, Baker, Charlie.

Mae West and W. C. Fields

96. Movie titles often contain a number, such as *The Magnificent Seven* or *Three Little Words*. See if you can supply the number that is missing from these motion pictures of the 1940s:

a. _____*Graves to Cairo*
b. _____*Jills in a Jeep*
c. _____ *Keys to Baldpate*
d. _____*Lessons from Madame La Zonga*

97. The sports world has always been full of colorful nicknames. Reaching back in time, see if you can recall the athletes who had the following sobriquet:

a. The Brat
b. The Toy Bulldog
c. The Flying Parson
d. The Splendid Splinter

98. Many commercial product slogans have become as much a part of Americana as our movies, old radio programs, and comic book heroes. See if you can identify the products that made the following famous:

a. "Hasn't scratched yet!"
b. "The ham what am!"
c. "Time to re-tire?"
d. "Covers the world!"

96.

a. *Five Graves to Cairo,* a 1943 film starring Franchot Tone and Anne Baxter

b. *Four Jills in a Jeep,* a 1944 musical featuring Carole Landis, Martha Raye, Jimmy Dorsey's Orchestra, Dick Haymes, Betty Grable, and Carmen Miranda

c. *Seven Keys to Baldpate,* a wonderful mystery film made in 1947 featuring Eduardo Ciannelli and Arthur Shields

d. *Six Lessons from Madame La Zonga,* a 1941 comedy with Leon Errol, Lupe Velez, and Shemp Howard of the Three Stooges.

97.

a. Eddie Stanky, who appeared in the World Series as a player for three different teams, the Brooklyn Dodgers, Boston Braves, and New York Giants

b. Mickey Walker, the world's welterweight boxing champion from 1922–26

c. Rev. Bob Richards, the Olympic pole vault champion in 1952 and again in 1956

d. Ted Williams, the six-time American League batting champion for the Boston Red Sox

98.

a. Bon Ami (the famous chick was created in 1901 for an ad but customers responded so enthusiastically to the chick that it was soon added to the package as a trademark)

b. Armour Ham

c. Fisk Tires (the sleepy child with a candle in one hand and a tire in the other was created by an 18-year-old advertising artist named Burr Giffen who thought of it one night in 1907 while lying in bed. He got up and made a rough sketch, and it eventually became the company's primary symbol.)

d. Sherwin-Williams Paint

99. A former Norwegian Minister of War collaborated with the Nazis during World War II and was so despised by his countrymen that his last name became a synonym for traitor. Who was he?

100. Babe Ruth's predecessor in right field for the New York Yankees is also a Hall of Famer...but not baseball. The pro *football* Hall of Fame. Who is he?

101. There were many famous horses in movie westerns. But few people can name the top thirteen movie western horses of all time. One that you are likely to overlook is a horse that usually appeared without a rider. See how many you can come up with.

a. Trigger
b. Silver
c. Silver (There were two horses named Silver!)
d. Topper
e. Tony
f. Champion
g. Goldie
h. Tarzan
i. Fritz
j. Rex
k. Buttermilk
l. White Flash
m. Rush

102. Here's an intriguing riddle. A man decides to go into business selling coconuts. He buys them for five dollars a dozen and sells them for three dollars a dozen. As a result of this, he becomes a millionaire. How is that possible?

99. Vidkun Quisling, who was imprisoned and then executed after the war.

100. George Halas, the beloved Papa Bear of Chicago's NFL team, the Bears.

101.
a. Roy Rogers
b. The Lone Ranger
c. Buck Jones
d. Hopalong Cassidy
e. Tom Mix
f. Gene Autry
g. Hoot Gibson
h. Ken Maynard
i. William S. Hart
j. This horse usually appeared on film without a rider and captured the bad guys by himself in movie serials of the 1930s.
k. Dale Evans (Mrs. Roy Rogers)
l. Tex Ritter
m. Lash LaRue

102. The man started out as a billionaire but he lost so much money in the coconut business that he became a millionaire.

103. Many of the great comic strip characters of the past used expressions that became familiar to readers. Try to remember who said the following:

a. Leapin' Lizards!
b. Great Scott!
c. Holy-Moley!
d. Well, blow me down!
e. Oh, Min!

104. More statues in the world have been put up in honor of one particular real person then anyone else. Who was the person?

105. The human body has given rise to nicknames for many celebrities. In fact one was known as

a. The Body. Who was she? Hint: she was an actress of the 1940s who made her film debut in Abbott and Costello's *Pardon My Sarong.*
b. The Lip
c. The Toe
d. And finally, not a celebrity but a comic strip villain known as The Head. In what popular strip did he appear often?

106. On a standard piano, only one *white* key does not touch a *black* key. Which key is it?

107. What story has been filmed more than any other work of fiction? To narrow it down, it is not *Robinson Crusoe* or *Gulliver's Travels*...not *A Christmas Carol* or *Alice in Wonderland.*

103.
a. Little Orphan Annie
b. Dick Tracy
c. Captain Marvel
d. Popeye
e. Andy Gump

104. Buddha

105.
a. Marie McDonald
b. Baseball manager Leo Durocher
c. NFL kicking star Lou Groza
d. Smilin' Jack

106. The highest C, the key at the extreme right of the keyboard

107. *Cinderella,* with *Hamlet* the second most filmed work of fiction

WWII gasoline rationing sticker

108. Here are the names of some well-known motion picture performers. However, they are more recognizable to us by another name. See if you can identify each of them.

a. Carl Switzer
b. William Boyd
c. Jerome Howard
d. Eddie Anderson

109. In the mid-1920s General Motors began making a car slightly more expensive than its Buick line but priced below Cadillac. What was this luxury car named?

110. A classic American automobile that was manufactured from 1899 to 1958 for a time had a memorable advertising slogan, "Ask the man who owns one." What was the car?

111. Here are some sports champions from the 1940s. See if you can name the sport each one competed in.

a. Ned Day
b. Mauri Rose
c. Frank Sedgman
d. Lloyd Mangrum
e. Frankie Sinkwich

112. Since Smith is such a common last name, it's no surprise that many people named Smith have been part of show business. There's Kate, famous for her rendition of "God Bless America." Joe Smith was part of the team of Smith and Dale. Maggie Smith won an Oscar in 1978 for her supporting role in *California Suite* after being named best actress in 1969 in *The Prime of Miss Jean Brodie*.. And you may remember Pete Smith, who produced and narrated a popular short subject for movie houses called *Pete Smith Specialties.* But there were only three Hollywood *stars* of the 1940s named Smith. Can you think of all three?

108.
a. Alfalfa of the *Our Gang* (Little Rascal) comedy shorts
b. Hopalong Cassidy (Boyd was the only actor ever to play that role)
c. Curly Howard of The Three Stooges
d. Rochester, Jack Benny's gravelly voiced valet who also appeared in such films as *Gone With The Wind, You Can't Take It With You, Green Pastures, Cabin in the Sky,* and *Topper Returns*

109. LaSalle

110. Packard

111.
a. Bowling
b. Auto racing
c. Tennis
d. Golf
e. College Football

112.
a. C. Aubrey Smith, the distinguished English actor
b. Alexis Smith, a leading lady
c. Kent Smith, star of such films as *Cat People, Hitler's Children,* and *The Spiral Staircase.*

113. For a very logical reason, one of these states does not belong in this list. It has something to do with the capital cities of the states. See if you can figure it out.
Missouri, Nevada, New York, Oklahoma, and Utah

114. Old-time radio had many husband-and-wife comedy teams such as George Burns and Gracie Allen. See if you can remember the real-life wife and partner of the following radio comedians:

a. Jack Benny
b. Fred Allen
c. Jim Jordan, better known as Fibber McGee
d. Goodman Ace, the co-star of "Easy Aces"

115. During Hollywood's Golden Age there were many performers whose first names were one of a kind. There was only one Tyrone (Power), one Cary (Grant), one major star named Clark (Gable), only one Myrna (Loy), and one Deanna (Durbin). But there were *two* leading ladies whose first name was Carole, two stars were known as Buster, and a pair of famous comedians shared the first name of Bert. Can you name them?

116. What famous names come to mind when you hear the following phrases:

a. The Songbird of the South
b. The Poet of the Piano
c. Old Number 98
d. "My Time Is Your Time"

117. Both France and Germany began World War II with defense lines that proved ineffective. France's stretched from Switzerland to Belgium along the border with Germany. The German counterpart faced it. What were those two lines called?

113. Only New York does not belong in the list. It is the only one whose capital (Albany) does not contain the word "city" (Jefferson City, Carson City, Oklahoma City, and Salt Lake City)

114.
a. Mary Livingstonc
b. Portland Hoffa
c. Marian Jordan, who played Molly McGee
d. Jane Ace, famous for her malapropisms such as: "The fly in the oatmeal," Congress is still in season," and "I've been working my head to the bone."

115. Carole Lombard, who was married to Clark Gable and died tragically in a plane crash, and Carole Landis, who took her own life at age 29. Buster Keaton, the silent movie comedian, and Buster Crabbe, who played Flash Gordon in the movie serials. Bert Lahr, the cowardly lion in *The Wizard of Oz,* and Bert Wheeler, half of the Wheeler and Woolsey team (Robert Woolsey was his partner).

116.
a. Kate Smith
b. Carmen Cavallaro, the great society music pianist and bandleader
c. Tom Harmon, who wore that number while starring for Michigan on the gridiron. He later became a prominent sportscaster on radio and TV
d. Rudy Vallee, the crooner, actor, and bandleader, always closed his radio show ("The Fleischmann Hour") singing "My Time Is Your Time."

117. The French called theirs the Maginot Line, while the German version was known as the Siegfried Line.

118. Can you identify the following names from World War II?

a. Leon Henderson
b. Donald Nelson
c. Husband Kimmel
d. Semyon Timoshenko
e. Draza Mihajlovic

119. There have been many Hollywood actresses named Shirley and Barbara and Elizabeth, but during the movies' Golden Age of the 1940s there was only one leading lady with each of the following names:

a. Merle
b. Alexis
c. Jeanette
d. Yvonne
Can you recall their last names?

120. Here are the numbers of some very famous street addresses. See if you can identify each one.

a. 79
b. Ten
c. 1600
d. 221B

121. There is a common eight-letter word nearly everyone is familiar with. The odd thing is that four of its eight letters are *F*s. What is the word?

122. The automobile Cadillac is named for an explorer. There are three extinct U.S. cars that also have the name of an explorer. How many can you think of?

118.

a. Head of the Office of Price Administration (OPA). The bureau was set up to regulate prices in the United States.

b. Head of the War Production Board, responsible for putting the U.S. economy on a war footing

c. Admiral in charge of the U.S. fleet that was attacked at Pearl Harbor

d. Russia's first World War II hero who commanded the armies that stopped the German attack on Moscow

e. Leader of Yugoslavian guerrillas who eventually fought against another guerrilla leader, Josip Broz Tito

119.

a. Merle Oberon

b. Alexis Smith

c. Jeanette MacDonald

d. Yvonne DeCarlo

120.

a. 79 Wistful Vista, the home of Fibber McGee and Molly

b. Number Ten Downing Street, the residence of British prime ministers

c. 1600 Pennsylvania Avenue, the address of the White House in Washington, D.C.

d. 221B Baker, where Sherlock Holmes lived

121. Riffraff

122. Hudson, DeSoto, and LaSalle

123. Some famous popular songs contain numbers. Try to recall the songs whose lyrics contain the following numbers:

a. 29
b. 49
c. 92
d. 105

124. Though the programs in this question have been off the dial for nearly half a dozen decades, we still remember some of the things we heard on them week after week. On what shows did we hear the following:

a. "I calls them the way I sees them"
b. A hospital bell followed by a woman's voice saying, "Dr. Brent, call surgery"
c. "I'm back in the saddle again, out where a friend is a friend"
d. Based "on the famous Metro-Goldwyn-Mayer motion picture series which brought to life to millions and reflected the common joys and tribulations of the average American family." (The script did use the awkward phrase "brought to life to millions.")

125. Every letter of the alphabet can be rhymed with an ordinary word in English except one. Which letter cannot be rhymed?

126. Hollywood in its Golden Years had only one superstar whose first name was Spencer (Tracy) and one with the name Tyrone (Power). See if you can recall the last name of the following stars of that era:

a. Deanna
b. Bonita
c. Mischa
d. Laird

123.
a. "Chattanooga Choo-Choo" (track 29)
b. Another train song, "On the Atchison, Topeka, and the Santa Fe" (engine number 49) or you might have come up with "Clementine" ("a miner 49er')
c. "The Christmas Song" ("kids from one to ninety-two")
d. "Young at Heart" ("If you should survive to a hundred and five")

124.
a. Red Skelton as Junior, the Mean Widdle Kid
b. "Road of Life," a medical soap opera that ran for 22 years from 1937–1959
c. Gene Autry's Melody Ranch, sponsored for its entire run from 1940–1956 (except for Autry's three years in service) by Wrigley's Doublemint Gum
d. "The Hardy Family," featuring Mickey Rooney as Andy Hardy

125. *H*

126.
a. Deanna Durbin, the brilliant singing star who retired while still very young
b. Bonita Granville, a popular child actress of the 1930s
c. Mischa Auer, a comedy performer remembered for his prominent eyes and wild gestures. He came from Russia after the Revolution
d. Laird Cregar, a heavyset character actor with roles in such films as *I Wake Up Screaming, Heaven Can Wait, The Lodger,* and *Hangover Square.* He died at the age of 28, cutting short a brilliant career.

127. In 1954 a former band singer with Jack Teagarden, Jimmy Dorsey, and Harry James recorded for Decca one of the best-selling songs of all time. It was America's number-one popular song for nine weeks, "Little Things Mean a Lot." Who was the endearing vocalist?

128. Body-builder Angelo Siciliano became famous after changing his name and advertising that he had once been a 97-pound weakling. Who was he?

129. "Strong legs run so that weak legs can walk" was the slogan of a once well-known athletic event. What was it?

130. Many actors of Radio's Golden Age were far better known by their character name than by their own. Who were the following:

a. Jim Jordan
b. Merwyn Bogue
c. Bill Comstock

131. A group of girls named Annette, Cécile, Émilie, Marie, and Yvonne attained instant fame in 1934. Can you identify them?

132. There was something unique about FDR cabinet members Henry L. Stimson (secretary of war) and Frank Knox (secretary of the navy). What was it?

127. Kitty Kallen

128. Charles Atlas

129. The now-defunct East-West Shrine college football game played in San Francisco

130.
a. Fibber McGee
b. Ish Kabibble (on "Kay Kyser's Kollege of Musical Knowledge")
c. Tizzie Lish (on "Al Pearce and His Gang")

131. The Dionne Quintuplets (delivered by Dr. Allan Roy Dafoe)

132. They were the only Republicans in the cabinet

New York World's Fair president Grover Whalen in 1939 with a 6939 A.D. time capsule

133. Youthful actors Leo Gorcey, Huntz Hall, Billy Halop, Bobby Jordan, Gabe Dell, and Bernard Punsley appeared together in dozens of movies. Can you recall any of the series they made?

134. The stars of two popular radio adventure programs as well as a string of "B" movies each had names starting with "B"–Boston and Bulldog. Can you complete the names of these fictional investigators?

135. When we recall the great dancers of the silver screen we think first of Fred and Ginger–Astaire and Rogers. See if you can recall the last names of these other great movie dancers:

a. Cyd
b. Marge and Gower
c. Gene
d. another Gene
e. Ann
f. Eleanor
g. Ray
h. Donald
i. Juliet
j. Three other dancers who became dramatic actors: James, Buddy, and George

136. Bob Eberly and Helen O'Connell were long associated with Jimmy Dorsey's orchestra. Try to recall the band most closely associated with the following vocalists:

a. Perry Como
b. Doris Day
c. Harry Babbitt
d. Ginny Simms
e. Rosemary Clooney
f. Bing Crosby

133. They appeared in movies as *The Dead End Kids*, *The Dead End Kids and Little Tough Guys*, *The East Side Kids*, and *The Bowery Boys*

134. Boston Blackie, Bulldog Drummond

135.
a. Charisse
b. Champion
c. Kelly
d. Nelson
e. Miller
f. Powell
g. Bolger
h. O'Connor
i. Prowse
j. Cagney, Ebsen, and Raft (George Murphy is also an acceptable answer)

136.
a. Ted Weems
b. Les Brown
c. Kay Kyser
d. also Kay Kyser
e. Tony Pastor
f. Paul Whitman

Kay Kyser on NBC's
"Kollege of Musical Knowledge"

137. Here are the names of some old ballparks in the major leagues. Try to name the city in which each was located:

a. Shibe Park
b. Briggs Stadium
c. Sportsman's Park
d. Hilltop Park
e. Griffith Stadium

138. "Let's return to those thrilling days of yesteryear." That, of course, is a line from the opening of "The Lone Ranger." On what radio programs did we hear the following?

a. A host who called himself "Your obedient servant"
b. A program that awarded a box of the sponsor's candy bars and "two tickets to next week's production" at the theater where the broadcast took place (the show moved from city to city)
c. "The story you are about to hear is true. Only the names have been changed to protect the innocent."
d. "Come in, come in, the door is open." Part of the opening of a well-known soap opera.

139. Here's a challenge for baseball fans. How many of these players can you identify from their feline nickname?

a. The Kitten
b. The Cat
c. The *Big* Cat

137.
a. Philadelphia
b. Detroit
c. St. Louis
d. New York (it's where the Giants played while the Polo Grounds was being rebuilt after fire destroyed the original Polo Grounds stadium)
e. Washington, D.C.

138.
a. Orson Welles called himself that on "The Mercury Theatre on the Air," the show that shocked broadcasting in 1938 with its presentation of "The War of the Worlds."
b. Dr. I.Q. (The candy and tickets were a consolation prize to contestants who failed to win a cash prize of silver dollars on the quiz)
c. The opening of "Dragnet"
d. Papa David (played by Ralph Locke) on "Life Can Be Beautiful," known in the trade as "Elsie Beebe" for LCBB

139.
a. Harvey Haddix
b. Harry Brecheen
c. Johnny Mize

140. An outfielder was nicknamed "Babe Ruth's Legs" because he filled in for the Bambino on so many occasions. The sub was never a big star in the majors, playing with the New York Yankees from 1929–1934 and for the Cincinnati Reds from 1935–1936. But he compiled a respectable .274 batting average in 744 games with 38 homeruns. He also appeared in the 1932 World Series with no at-bats. He later concentrated on the sport of golf and was one of the brightest stars on the pro tour. What was his name?

141. In 1940 a political committee was organized to oppose United States aid to nations fighting Axis aggression.The members included General Robert E. Wood, Charles Lindbergh, Burton K. Wheeler, Gerald P. Nye, and John T. Flynn. Can you recall the name of the committee?

142. Popular, Super, Ace, Tip-Top, Action, Whiz, Tops, Detective, All-Star, All-American, Nickel. These were some of the best-known names in their field in the 1930s and 1940s. What were they?

143. Here are some terms used in various sports. Try to figure out what each sport is.

a. strike, tag, and rover
b. period, face-off, and icing
c. boom, bridle, and spinnaker
d. bowler, striker, and crease

144. Fritz Kuhn led a group founded in Chicago in 1932 known as Friends of the New Germany. Its aim was to encourage the Nazis in Germany and spy on the United States while engaging in pro-Nazi propaganda. The group later changed its name in order to attract new members, and it grew to some twenty thousand, most of them in New York City. What was the group's new name?

140. Sammy Byrd

141. America First Committee

142. They were all titles of comic books

143.
a. softball (rover is the name often applied to the tenth man or shortfielder)
b. ice hockey
c. sailing
d. cricket

144. German-American Bund

A common sight on movie theater screens

145. Had the Republicans succeeded in winning the White House in the 1940 presidential election, neither the president nor vice-president, as it turned out, would have survived a full term. Thus, whoever had been chosen as secretary of state would have assumed the presidency under the existing succession laws. Can you recall the names of the two GOP candidates for president and vice-president who lost to the Roosevelt-Wallace ticket in 1940?

146. Though not a member of the "America First Committee," a fiery orator of the 1930s strongly supported its goals and founded his own similar organization—The Committee of One Million—which advocated isolationism as well as opposition to Communism. He campaigned with Huey Long, supported Union Party presidential candidate William Lemke in 1936, and worked closely with the "Radio Priest," Father Charles E. Coughlin. Who was this firebrand who happened to have two middle initials?

147. During the Golden Age of comic strips, many of the Sunday strips featured what was known as a "Bottom Piece," a separate strip running directly under the main story. Try to recall the strip that each of the following was featured under:

a. "Looie," a diminutive lawyer who was constantly flabbergasted by the judge or a client and, as a result, in the final panel seemed to be close to fainting
b. "Phil Fumble," the wavy-haired much shorter boyfriend of the star of the main strip
c. "Kitty Higgins," a little girl who was a friend of a small boy who appeared regularly in the main strip.
d. "Maw Green," an elderly woman with an Irish brogue who was a sort of homespun philosopher

145. Wendell Willkie (1892–1944) and Charles McNary (1874–1944)

146. Gerald L. K. Smith (Gerald Lyman Kenneth Smith)

147.
a. "Winnie Winkle"
b. "Fritzi Ritz"
c. "Moon Mullins" (Kayo was Kitty's friend)
d. "Little Orphan Annie"

1940 GOP presidential
candidate Wendell Willkie

148. Here are the real names of some sports celebrities. Try to identify them.

a. Arnold Cream, the heavyweight boxing champion in 1951 and 1952
b. John Paveskovich, a shortstop widely publicized for holding onto the ball too long while taking a relay in the 1946 World Series during Enos Slaughter's mad dash from first base to score the winning run in game seven.
c. Cornelius McGillicuddy, a famous baseball manager
d. Walker Smith, a boxer who became welterweight champion of the world and then middleweight king

149. The first chairman of the House Un-American Activities Committee represented Texas for a total of twenty years (1931–1945 and 1953–1959). Though a Democrat, he fought against many New Deal programs and claimed Communists were controlling some key United States institutions. Who was this headline-making congressman?

150. Here are the real names of some well-known movie stars. See if you can come up with the names that we remember them by:

a. Spangler Arlington Brugh
b. Archibald Leach
c. Leonard Slye
d. Sarah Jane Fulks
e. Julius Garfinkle

151. The Ivy League has had three Heisman Trophy winners, two from one college and one from another. Can you think of the two schools that supplied Heisman winners?

148.
a. Jersey Joe Walcott
b. Johnny Pesky
c. Connie Mack
d. Sugar Ray Robinson

149. Martin Dies, Jr.

150.
a. Robert Taylor
b. Cary Grant
c. Roy Rogers
d. Jane Wyman
e. John Garfield

151. Larry Kelley of Yale, 1936; Clinton Frank of Yale, 1937; Dick Kazmaier of Princeton, 1951

152. Hollywood turned out many highly publicized films during its Golden Age. See if you can recall the title of each of the following from a brief description.

a. The story of an encounter between Billy the Kid and Doc Holliday. Howard Hughes withheld the film from release for three years to garner publicity as censor boards argued about Jane Russell's part in it.

b. A sensational horror film of 1942 starring Simone Simon. A publicity blurb says "Woman or leopard? She was *both*, for the curse was in her kiss."

c. The definitive World War II film about a middle-class English family learning to cope with war. Greer Garson and Teresa Wright won two of the film's six Academy Awards. It also starred Walter Pidgeon and Richard Ney.

d. One of the most heavily advertised films in history, starring Joan Crawford as a housewife-turned-actress who loses control of her ungrateful daughter who is competing for the love of the same man. The daughter was played by Ann Blyth.

153. Willie Hoppe and Casey Tibbs were two of the most successful champions in United States sports history. They were not from baseball, football, basketball, swimming, track, or boxing. What did they do?

154. Here are some characters from the old movie serials. See if you can identify the serials they were in.

a. Ivan Shark, Icky, and Joyce
b. Professor Parker, Mary Randolph, and detective Nayland Smith
c. Mike McGurk, The Lame One, and Junior
d. Billy, Rahman Bar, and The Scorpion

152.
a. "The Outlaw"
b. "Cat People"
c. "Mrs. Miniver"
d. "Mildred Pierce"

153. Hoppe was a billiards expert, and Tibbs was a rodeo performer

154.
a. *Captain Midnight*, which featured the same characters on the radio serial
b. *The Drums of Fu Manchu* (Nayland Smith was the brilliant detective who pursued the evil Fu Manchu in the books and on screen)
c. Dick Tracy
d. Captain Marvel

Tom Tyler as Captain Marvel
in the 1941 Republic Pictures
movie serial (12 episodes)

155. According to the Bible, who cut Samson's hair? Careful now. This question is not as easy as it may appear to be.

156. Returning to vintage radio, try to recall whom listeners would find at the following addresses:

a. The Eight-to-the Bar Ranch
b. The A-1 Detective Agency
c. The Little Theater Off Times Square
d. Painted Valley

157. An obscure ABC radio show for young people ran only two years but to this day some oldtime listeners recall its familiar opening sequence in which a bullet ricochets. The dialogue went: "There he goes! Get him!" After the ricochet we heard: "Got him! Deeeeead center!" What was the name of this program set on the frontier shortly after the Civil War?

158. Middle names are often very important. For example, the name William Harrison may not register with us, but William Henry Harrison instantly brings to mind a United States president. The same holds true for Robert Stevenson instead of Robert Louis Stevenson. See if you can come up with the full name of the following well-known people from just their middle name:

a. Lind, a longtime radio-TV personality who often appeared with his wife, Mary
b. Charles, a popular baritone in the 1940s
c. Everett, a well-known movie character actor
d. May, a character actress of the silver screen who often played a stern but warm-hearted spinster.

155. Surprisingly it was not Delilah who cut Samson's hair. In the Book of Judges it says Delilah sent for a man to shave Samson's head.

156.
a. The Andrews Sisters
b. Jack, Doc, and Reggie of "I Love a Mystery"
c. Mr. First Nighter
d. Red Ryder

157. Tennessee Jed

158.
a. Peter Lind Hayes
b. John Charles Thomas
c. Edward Everett Horton
d. Edna May Oliver

Labor leader John L. Lewis

159. Let's return to the aircraft of World War II. You may recall that Lockheed was the principal builder of the P-38 Lightning and North American the P-51 Mustang. Who built the following planes?

a. The P-40 Warhawk, used so effectively by the Flying Tigers in China
b. The P-47 Thunderbolt, noted for both aerial combat and ground support
c. The famous Navy plane known as the Hellcat
d. The fighter plane that brought glory to Marine pilots, the F4U Corsair

160. Many American automobiles were named for men. Sometimes it was for the maker himself, sometimes for famous men in history. Try to identify the make of car named for men with the following first names:

a. Powel
b. Abraham
c. Benjamin
d. Brothers John and Horace
e. Antoine
f. Louis
g. Errett
h. Hernando
i. René
j. Preston
k. Brothers Henry and Clem

161. One of the greatest of all comic book heroes was a crime-fighter who went by the alias of Alan Scott and said in his oath: "In brightest day, in blackest night, no evil shall escape my sight. Let those who worship evil's might beware my power." Who was he?

159.
a. Curtiss
b. Republic
c. Grumman
d. Chance-Vought

160.
a. Crosley
b. Lincoln
c. Franklin
d. Dodge
e. Cadillac
f. Chevrolet
g. Cord
h. DeSoto
i. LaSalle
j. Tucker
k. Studebaker

161. The Green Lantern

Flying Tigers P-40 Warhawk

162. Here are the last names of some celebrities of the 1940s. The people in each group all shared the same *first* name. See if you can come up with those first names.

a. Young, Kerr, Rogers, and Rich
b. Taylor, Moses, Montgomery, and LaFollette
c. Powell, Roosevelt, and Holm

163. Here is a list of seven brothers who made their family name one of the most famous in American history. Their first names were Albert, Alfred, August, Charles, Henry, John, and Otto. What was was their famous *last* name?

164. Let's try to recall some of the old automobiles that are no longer being made. From the various models, identify the make:

a. Pacer, Corsair, Bermuda, and Villager
b. Commodore, Big Boy, Hornet, and Wasp
c. Rambler, Ambassador, Lafayette, Statesman
d. Superba, Marathon, Town Custom

165. Supermarket shelves are loaded with various brands of soft drinks. What do you think is the oldest one? (Hint: it's not Coca-Cola or Pepsi.)

166. Now we return to the old days of Hollywood to try to identify some well-known screen personalities by their nicknames.

a. Cuddles
b. Smiley
c. Big Boy
d. Deadpan

167. One of the most beloved of all comic strip characters was a little boy who slept in a drawer. Can you name him and the strip in which he appeared?

162.
a. Buddy
b. Robert
c. Eleanor

163. Ringling (the famous Ringling Brothers of circus fame)

164.
a. Edsel, which was made from 1958–1960
b. Hudson (the company was named for one of its founders, Joseph L. Hudson, who ran a huge chain of department stores in Detroit)
c. Nash
d. Checker (a line of cars for the public was built in 1959 after the company had been in business for 37 years making taxis and airport limousines)

165. Dr. Pepper, which dates back to 1885

166.
a. S. Z. Sakall, a Hungarian character actor who did not speak English for his first Hollywood film but said the words anyway
b. Smiley Burnette
c. Guinn Williams
d. Virginia O'Brien, who sang emotional lyrics with no facial expression as a comic bit

167. Kayo in "Moon Mullins"

168. For a brief time the nonsensical comment "Greetings Gate!" swept the United States. It originated on a popular radio show and was uttered by a well-loved mustachioed comedian in the supporting cast. Can you name the show and the comedian?

169. Here are some catch-phrases from vintage radio. Try to identify the program on which each was heard.

a. "Expense account, item one." (This was the last major network drama on radio, and the star of the show said the foregoing each week.)
b. "Would you like to be _____?" Can you fill in the blank, which was the title of the show that starred Jack Bailey as M.C.?
c. "Gosh all fishhooks, Jack."

170. Many of America's greatest singers appeared on a long-running program that began in 1928. Among them were Richard Crooks, Margaret Speaks, Gladys Swarthout, Lawrence Tibbett, Lauritz Melchior, Rose Bampton, and John Charles Thomas. The longtime announcer was Hugh James, and the familiar theme song was "If I Could Tell You," written by the wife of the man who owned the company that sponsored each broadcast. What was the program called?

171. Not many vintage radio shows had a Latin title, but a popular quiz show did. It featured at first Parks Johnson and Jerry Belcher. Wally Butterworth and Warren Hull were among later M.C.s. Can you think of the program's name?

172. There are a number of songs that we associate with a particular college. Try to name the school that uses the following:

a. "The Victors"
b. "The Rouser"
c. "On the Banks of the Old Raritan"
d. The melody of "I've Been Working on the Railroad"

168. Jerry Colonna on "The Bob Hope Show"

169.
a. "Yours Truly, Johnny Dollar"
b. "Queen For a Day"
c. "Jack Armstrong" (it was said often by Billy Fairfield, Jack's cousin)

170. "The Voice of Firestone"

171. "Vox Pop"

172.
a. Michigan
b. Minnesota
c. Rutgers
d. Texas

173. Here are names of five Hollywood stars who have something in common with one another. Here's a big hint: it has something to do with a well-known movie award. What is the common link among Walter Huston, Kirk Douglas, Judy Garland, Ryan O'Neal, and Henry Fonda?

174. They were not as well known as Superman and Captain Marvel, but two other comic book heroes with legions of fans also turned up in movie serials. One was a patriotic man of action who wore a flowing cape and gloves, a diamond emblem on his chest, and on his belt a large V for Victory with the Morse Code symbol of three dots and a dash. The other was even more colorfully attired in a striking red, white, and blue outfit. In the comics he was Steve Rogers in civilian life, but in the movie serials he was a district attorney named Grant Gardner. Can you name these two superheroes?

175. Here is the last line of a very famous document. Try to identify it. "If I transgress it and swear falsely, may the opposite of all this be my lot."

176. Here are some military mottoes. Try to identify the group each represents.

a. Semper Fidelis
b. Semper Paratus
c. Can Do

177. According to an exhaustive study of Hollywood movies, the sentence most often used in them has been a five-word sentence beginning with "Let's." Can you figure out what the sentence is?

173. Each had a child who won an Academy Award: John Huston, Michael Douglas, Liza Minnelli, Tatum O'Neal, and Jane Fonda

174. Spy Smasher, Captain America

175. The Hippocratic Oath

176.
a. U.S. Marine Corps (it means Always Faithful)
b. U.S. Coast Guard (Always Ready)
c. The Seabees (the fabulous group that took its name from the initials of its actual name, Construction Battalion)

177. "Let's get out of here."

178. Here are the real names of some famous movie stars of the past. See if you can come up with the names we remember them by.

a. Virginia McMath, a dancer
b. Harlean Carpentier, an actress
c. Joseph Levitch, a comedian
d. Arthur Jefferson, a comedian

179. Many big band fans recall "Ciribiribin" as Harry James's theme song and "I'm Getting Sentimental Over You" for Tommy Dorsey. Try to name the big bands that used the following songs for their themes.

a. "Rhapsody in Blue"
b. "Thinking of You"
c. "When My Baby Smiles At Me"
d. "Sugar Blues"
e. "Tonight We Love"

180. There was only one internationally famous comedian whose last name was Benny and only one named Berle. But five unrelated comedy stars share the same last name. Can you think of it?

181. A famous candy was invented the very year the *Titanic* sunk. This may sound like a frivolous question to ask what the name of the candy is, but when you know the answer you will realize it does indeed make sense to ask. What is the candy?

178.
a. Ginger Rogers
b. Jean Harlow
c. Jerry Lewis
d. Stan Laurel

179.
a. Paul Whiteman
b. Kay Kyser
c. Ted Lewis
d. Clyde McCoy
e. Freddy Martin

180. Allen (think of Fred, Gracie, Marty, Steve, and Woody)

181. Life Savers

Duke Ellington

182. Some of the most memorable films of all time were biographies. Many actors have portrayed Abraham Lincoln, but Raymond Massey survives as the quintessential performance. Try to name the actor most closely associated with the following:

a. Lou Gehrig
b. Louis Pasteur
c. Sigmund Freud
d. Sergeant York
e. Cole Porter
f. George M. Cohan
g. Benito Mussolini
h. Andrew Johnson
i. Woodrow Wilson
j. Vernon and Irene Castle

183. Here's an interesting word. It's only five letters long, but when you drop the last four letters it's still pronounced the same. What can that word be?

184. Everyone wants to be first, and we often forget who was second. Button Gwinnett was second to John Hancock in signing the Declaration of Independence. Saturn is huge enough to be the second largest planet in our solar system behind Jupiter. See if you can come up with the runner-up among the following:

a. Chinese is the most widely spoken language in the world. What's second?
b. Russia is the biggest country on earth in area. What's number two?
c. The Nile is the world's longest river. What's second?
d. The largest living land animal is the elephant. What is second largest?

182.
a. Gary Cooper
b. Paul Muni
c. Montgomery Clift
d. Gary Cooper
e. Cary Grant
f. James Cagney
g. Jack Oakie (in *The Great Dictator* with Charlie Chaplin as Adolf Hitler)
h. Van Heflin
i. Alexander Knox
j. Fred Astaire and Ginger Rogers

183. Queue

184.
a. English
b. Canada
c. the Amazon
d. the rhinoceros

185. Fanny Brice as Baby Snooks and comedian Frank Morgan got most of the laughs on radio's "Maxwell House Coffee Time." But when Snooks left the show another comedienne came on board playing Morgan's niece. Her trademark line became "I said it and I'm glad!" and it was widely repeated across the United States by listeners. Who was this long-forgotten radio star?

186. Upon his retirement from being the world's greatest detective, Sherlock Holmes supposedly took up a new profession. It had to do with a type of animal, and for a Holmesian type of clue, the profession is a nine-letter word of which five of the letters are *Es*. What was Sherlock's new profession?

187. "Your Hit Parade" featured many vocalists during its 24-year run on network radio. One of the female singers was married to the show's announcer, Andre Baruch, and decades later they were a broadcast twosome. Can you think of her name?

188. Here is a list of famous brothers. What are their last names?

a. Walker and Morton
b. Al, Harry, and Jim
c. William and Andrew
d. A quartet of Hollywood brothers: Albert, Harry, Jack, and Samuel

189. One of America's best-loved comic strips featured a henpecked husband who loved corned beef and had to dodge flying rolling pins tossed by his wife. What was the strip's title?

190. Ten of our states are named for Indian tribes. See how many you can come up with.

185. Cass Daley

186. Beekeeper

187. Bea Wain

188.
a. Cooper (catcher and pitcher team for the St. Louis Cardinals)
b. Ritz (The Ritz Brothers were a zany comedy team in movies of the 1930s and 1940s. Their theme song was "Thanks a Million.")
c. Smith (The famous Smith Brothers of cough drop fame, also known as Trade and Mark.)
d. Warner (The Warner Brothers founded their motion picture studio in 1923.)

189. "Bringing Up Father" (popularly known as "Jiggs and Maggie")

190. Alabama, Arkansas, Illinois, Iowa, Kansas, Michigan, Missouri, North Dakota, South Dakota, and Utah

191. On which program did M.C. Ben Grauer shout out, "Hold it, Horace. Stop the music!" to bandleader Horace Heidt when a contestant was on the phone trying for a prize?

192. Who is the only person named to both the baseball and pro football halls of fame?

193. What is the maximum number of bids, including passes, in a hand of contract bridge?

194. Here is a list of the most filmed fictional characters in history. Robin Hood is number eight; Charlie Chan is seventh; Zorro sixth; Hopalong Cassidy number five; Tarzan fourth. Can you name the top three?

195. The comic strip "Tim Tyler's Luck" was created by Lyman Young, whose brother drew an even more popular strip. And the creator of "Joe Palooka," Ham Fisher, had a brother who drew a better-known strip. What were the other strips?

196. Something geographical links all these celebrities. Try to figure out what it is. Mary Pickford, Jay Silverheels, Art Linkletter, Fay Wray, Raymond Burr, Raymond Massey, Deanna Durbin (some more recent people could be included, such as Lorne Greene, Monty Hall, Rich Little, and William Shatner).

197. A very popular children's radio program used to begin with the theme song, "Hello, nephews, nieces, mine... I'm glad to see you look so fine. How's Papa? How's Mama? But tell me first just how *you* are. I've many, many things to tell you on the radio." Can you recall the program?

191. "Pot O'Gold"

192. Cal Hubbard, a baseball umpire and NFL player for nine seasons

193. Surprisingly, 316. It would come from an unrealistic situation of starting with three passes, one club, two passes, double, two passes, redouble, two passes, two diamonds, two passes, etc.

194. Frankenstein's monster is number three, Dracula second, and most filmed of all is Sherlock Holmes.

195. Chic Young did "Blondie," and Bud Fisher did "Mutt and Jeff"

196. They were all born in Canada

197. Uncle Don

198. One of Hollywood's most celebrated film comedians used hornrim glasses with no lenses in them as a trademark. His greatest successes were silent movies such as *The Freshman* and *Safety Last,* in which he hung from the hands of a Roman-numeral clock high over city traffic. After retiring he became national head of the Shriners. Who was this memorable comedian?

199. Oldtime radio featured two "Beulahs." One was a black maid played originally by a white man, first with Fibber McGee and later on her (his) own show. But there was another Beulah that was not a person. Can you figure that one out?

200. There are only six common words in English that contain a double *V.* How many can you think of?

201. Of the hundreds of characters in nursery rhymes, one name is used far more than any other. Can you guess what it is?

202. How's your sense of geography? Brazil is such a vast country that it touches every other South American nation except two. What are the only two whose borders do not touch Brazil?

203. Among the characters appearing in a popular adventure comic strip were Sable, Swizzle Stick, Downwind Jaxon, and Fat Stuff. What was the strip?

204. Hal Foster, Harold Gray, Sidney Smith, Carl Ed (pronounced *eed*), Carl Anderson, and Ernie Bushmiller may not have been household names in the 1930s and 1940s, but their creations certainly were. What was their line of work?

198. Harold Lloyd

199. "Beulah the Buzzer," which sounded on "Truth or Consequences" when a contestant failed to answer a question correctly. Most of the time contestants preferred to get it wrong so they would "pay the consequences." That meant they would then take part in some zany stunt.

200. Divvies, divvy, flivver, revved, savvy, and skivvies (there is also a British word navvy referring to an unskilled laborer, but it is not a common word)

201. Jack, as in Jack and Jill, Jack and the Beanstalk, Jack Be Nimble, The House That Jack Built, Little Jack Horner, and so on.

202. Chile and Ecuador

203. "Smilin' Jack" (created by Zack Mosley)

204. They all drew and wrote comic strips ("Prince Valiant," "Little Orphan Annie," "The Gumps," "Harold Teen," "Henry," and "Fritzi Ritz" [also "Nancy"])

Fanny Brice as "Baby Snooks"

205. Among the heroes of movies, radio, and comic strips in the 1930s and 1940s were Hop Harrigan, Captain Midnight, Smilin' Jack, Tailspin Tommy, Jimmy Allen, The Sparrow and The Hawk, and Ace Drummond. What was their common occupation?

206. Bob Eberly and his younger brother Ray Eberle (who kept the original spelling) were both popular vocalists with two of the most famous orchestras of the Big Band era. Which two bands?

207. When Frank Sinatra left Tommy Dorsey's band to go solo, he was replaced by the same singer who took over for him when he left Harry James earlier. Who was the replacement?

208. One of the most popular songs of the 1940s was a simple tune called "Love Somebody." It featured a male and female vocalist on a 1948 record for Columbia. Can you recall the singers?

209. Harlow Wilcox was one of the best-known voices of Radio's Golden Age. He was the longtime announcer on a popular comedy show that, in turn, had a longtime sponsor. What was the progam, and who sponsored it?

210. So-called "Bottom Pieces" ran under many popular Sunday comic strips. They were by the same author as the main strip above them and were generally humorous even if the main strip was adventure. They were usually brief, only three or four panels, and sometimes used characters who appeared above them. Try to recall the main strip that ran above the following:

a. Herby
b. Cigarette Sadie
c. Jinglet
d. Cicero's Cat
e. Spooky
f. Corky

205. They were all aviators

206. Bob was with Jimmy Dorsey, while Ray sang for Glenn Miller

207. Dick Haymes

208. Doris Day and Buddy Clark

209. "Fibber McGee and Molly," sponsored by Johnson's Wax. Wilcox was the first show announcer to be integrated into the story line.

210.
a. "Smitty"
b. "Dick Tracy"
c. "Sweeney and Son"
d. "Mutt and Jeff"
e. "Smokey Stover"
f. "Gasoline Alley"

211. During the Big Band era, vocalists often attained fame as great or greater than the bandleaders. What renowned orchestra featured at various times Helen Ward, Martha Tilton, Helen Forrest, and Peggy Lee?

212. Vocalist Herb Jeffries was succeeded by Al Hibbler, the blind singer, with one of America's great swing bands. With another famous band of the era, Jimmy Rushing ("Mr. Five by Five") was followed by Joe Williams. Can you name the two orchestra leaders?

213. In January 1942 Mrs. Clark Gable, herself one of Hollywood's top stars, was killed in a TWA airliner crash near Las Vegas on a flight from New York's La Guardia. She was returning from a trip to promote the sale of defense bonds. Who was the 32-year-old actress?

214. No actor was better at playing introspective roles than a sensitive performer who was thrice nominated for an Oscar while appearing in such films as *The Search, Red River, The Heiress, A Place in the Sun, From Here to Eternity,* and *Freud.* Can you identify this moody performer?

215. In 1936 a long-running comic strip began that featured a masked crusader for justice who lived in the African jungle and continued a tradition passed from father to son since the sixteenth century. His costume was purple and he had a wolf dog named Devil at his side. Can you identify him?

216. In 1949 Freddy Martin's orchestra recorded "I've Got a Lovely Bunch of Coconuts." The record helped launch the career of the band's new vocalist, who later became a popular TV talk-show host, TV producer, and entrepreneur. Who was the singer?

211. Benny Goodman

212. Duke Ellington, Count Basie

213. Carole Lombard

214. Montgomery Clift

215. The Phantom

216. Merv Griffin

217. During World War II a popular blonde movie actress wore her long hair in a "peek-a-boo" style hanging over her right eye. A government agency asked her to quit wearing it that way because many women, imitating her style, were catching their hair in factory machinery. Who was the famous movie star?

218. A singer from Chicago named Frank Lovecchio changed his name and recorded such number-one hits as "That Lucky Old Sun," "Mule Train," and "The Cry of the Wild Goose." Can you identify him?

219. A supporting actor in Hollywood films was the father of an actress who was the third to play the mother role on TV's "Lassie" series. The Canadian-born actor wrote the words for the popular song "The World Is Waiting for the Sunrise." Who was he?

220. Theme songs were important in the days of oldtime radio. On what shows were the following songs used as themes?

a. "When the Moon Comes Over the Mountain"
b. "Friendship"
c. "Love Nest" (actually used on two different programs)
d. "Thinking of You"

221. Here are some groups of well-known baseball players who all played the same position. Try to name the position each quartet played.

a. Nick Etten, George McQuinn, Joe Kuhel, and Phil Cavarretta
b. George Pipgras, Schoolboy Rowe, Bob Purkey, and Don Bessent
c. Frankie Hayes, Rollie Hemsley, Clyde Kluttz, and Paul Richards
d. Lucky Lohrke, Whitey Kurowski, Ken Keltner, and Jimmy Collins

217. Veronica Lake

218. Frankie Laine

219. Gene Lockhart

220.
a. "The Kate Smith Show"
b. "My Friend Irma"
c. "Burns and Ellen"; "Ethel and Albert"
d. "Kay Kyser's Kollege of Musical Knowledge"

221.
a. first base
b. pitcher
c. catcher
d. third base

222. Here are some once familiar catch-phrases from Radio's Golden Age. Try to recall the show on which we heard them.

a. "Honest to my grandma, son!"
b. "Heigh-ho, everybody!"
c. "Hello, Joe. Al."
d. "The White Rabbit Line...jumps anywhere, anytime"

223. During Hollyywood's heyday, there were many famous child stars. Try to name the following youthful performers.

a. Bonita, who was nominated for an Academy Award in 1936 for her role in *These Three*
b. Scotty, who played Al Jolson as a youth in *The Jolson Story*
c. Butch, who made an impact with his first movie, *The Human Comedy*, at the age of six
d. Johnny, who is remembered chiefly for a running role in a popular movie series.

224. In 1948 an automobile was introduced with the slogan "The Most Completely New Car in Fifty Years." Only fifty of them were produced. The builder was tried for mail fraud and acquitted. What was the make of car?

225. Sherlock Holmes solved his cases with Dr. Watson at his side. Dick Tracy had Pat Patton. The Shadow could count on his friend and companion, the lovely Margot Lane. Here are some other famous helpers from movies and the comics. Try to figure out the person they assisted.

a. Kato
b. Lothar
c. California and Lucky

226. There are eight capital cities in the United States that have two words in their name and one that has three. How many of them can you think of?

222.
a. Doc Long of "I Love a Mystery"
b. Rudy Vallee on "The Rudy Vallee Show," also known as "The Fleischmann Hour"
c. That was the street hustler Al talking to his pal on the telephone on "My Friend Irma"
d. The opening to "Coast-to-Coast On a Bus"

223.
a. Granville
b. Beckett
c. Jenkins
d. Sheffield, who played "Boy" in the Tarzan films with Johnny Weissmuller and later starred as Bomba in another series

224. Tucker

225.
a. The faithful valet of the Green Hornet
b. Clad in his leopard skin suit and a fez on his head, Lothar ably assisted Mandrake the Magician
c. They worked alongside cowboy hero Hopalong Cassidy

226. Baton Rouge, Carson City, Des Moines, Jefferson City, Little Rock, Oklahoma City, Santa Fe, and St. Paul. The three-word capital city is Salt Lake City.

227. What do these political personalities all have in common? Frank Knox, Charles McNary, John Bricker, John J. Sparkman, Estes Kefauver

228. Try to identify these classic movies from a brief description of each.

a. A 1945 movie about a handsome young man who vows to surrender his soul if he can remain youthful while his portrait grows older and hideous.
b. A 1942 film about life in a supposedly fine town with undercurrents that reveal its ugly side when a doctor unnecessarily amputates the legs of a young man he disapproves of as a suitor for his daughter. It featured Robert Cummings, Ann Sheridan, and Ronald Reagan.
c. The spine-tingling tale of an invalid who overhears on the telephone two men plotting to kill her. The role won an Academy Award nomination for Barbara Stanwyck. Burt Lancaster played her treacherous husband.

229. See if you can identify the games in which the following terms are used.

a. dummy, rubber, and vulnerable
b. chance, house, and jail
c. history, roll again, and wedge
d. kitchen, knife, and mustard

230. With what heroic figures did the following work?

a. Lois Lane
b. Margot Lane
c. Smiley Burnette
d. Dale Arden
e. Red Pennington

227. They were all unsuccessful candidates for vice-president. The first three were Republicans and the other two Democrats.

228.
a. *The Picture of Dorian Gray*
b. *Kings Row*
c. *Sorry, Wrong Number*

229.
a. Bridge
b. Monopoly
c. Trivial Pursuit
d. Clue

230.
a. Superman
b. The Shadow
c. Gene Autry's sidekick in many westerns (but you're also correct if you answered Charles Starrett, a cowboy star who had been a football player)
d. Dale was at the side of space adventurer Flash Gordon in the movie serials, radio, and comic strips
e. Aide to Don Winslow of the Navy

WITHIN THIS VAIL

OF TOIL

AND SIN

YOUR HEAD GROWS BALD

BUT NOT YOUR CHIN

BURMA SHAVE

SLOW DOWN, PA

SAKES ALIVE

MA MISSED SIGNS

FOUR

AND FIVE

BURMA SHAVE

Burma-Shave signs with witty verses amused travelers along U.S. highways from 1929-1965.

Charles Atlas

231. Dick Tracy was a detective. So was Dan Dunn. Mandrake was a magician, and Steve Canyon a pilot. What comic strip characters had the following occupations?

a. A fireman whose strip often featured a sign saying "Notary Sojac" and the ears flying off people and labeled "engine ears" or "mountaineers," or such.
b. A policeman whose name was the same as a powerful drink.
c. A boxer with a manager named Knobby Walsh.
d. A caveman who worked with a scientist who had a time machine. His name was Dr. Wonmug.

232. Let's return to Radio's Golden Age. From brief descriptions of some programs of that era, try to figure out the name of the show.

a. A drama about a physician, played by Danish actor Jean Hersholt. It was the only show on network radio where the audience wrote the scripts.
b. The adventures of an elderly woman who operated a lumberyard in the town of Rushville Center. It was sponsored for years by Oxydol.
o. A children's daytime adventure serial featuring "America's Ace of the Airwaves." The flying hero identified his airplane as CX-4.
d. The primetime adventures of a detective known as a master of disguise who used his art to apprehend criminals. He was known as Mister _____, after a type of animal.

231.
a. Smokey Stover
b. Mickey Finn
c. Joe Palooka
d. Alley Oop

232.
a. "Dr. Christian"
b. "Ma Perkins"
c. "Hop Harrigan"
d. "Mr. Chameleon"

Ginger Rogers and Fred Astaire

233. Here are brief descriptions of three of the greatest films of Hollywood's Golden Age. Try to name the movies.

a. The tale of a reporter and an heiress who fall in love on a rural bus trip. It was the first film to win all five major Oscars for actor, actress, picture, director, and screenplay. It starred Clark Gable and Claudette Colbert.
b. A milestone film dealing with New York City slums starring Joel McCrea and Humphrey Bogart. It introduced a group of youngsters who went on to star in 85 other films playing similar roles.
c. The chilling story of a jealous woman who becomes involved in murder. Gene Tierney played the beautiful evil woman who is married to Cornel Wilde.

234. There are a number of first names from World War II that we identify with Allied heroes: Dwight, Winston, Douglas, and Omar for Eisenhower, Churchill, MacArthur, and Bradley. But how about some from the Axis side? Try to provide the last names of these Axis figures of World War II.

a. Vidkun
b. Pierre
c. Erwin
d. Pietro

235. Few people will remember a radio program called "Life with Luigi." It was about a group of Italian immigrants who settled in Chicago and was done in dialect. Audiences and critics alike loved it, and much of the credit for the show's success properly went to the actor who played Luigi. Ironically the star himself was of Irish extraction. He was in many movies, including *Beau Geste,* and was twice nominated for an Academy Award. Who was this master of dialect?

233.
a. *It Happened One Night*
b. *Dead End*
c. *Leave Her to Heaven*

234.
a. Quisling, a Norwegian Nazi collaborator whose name became a synonym for traitor
b. Laval, the premier of Vichy France
c. Rommel, German Field Marshal during World War II known as the Desert Fox. He was later forced to commit suicide by Hitler.
d. Badoglio, the Italian military leader in Ethiopia and later chief of staff. He resigned to protest Italy's entry into World War II and in 1943 arranged the surrender of Italy to the Allied armies.

235. J. Carrol Naish

236. You may have noticed that in an ordinary deck of cards the Jack of Hearts and the Jack of Spades are one-eyed. So how many eyes of Jacks will you find in a deck? (Careful now.)

237. Forty number-one hit records, all by the same vocalist! That incredible mark was set by a versatile performer who starred in films and on the radio. His first number-one hit was "Out of Nowhere," and his last was "Now Is the Hour." Can you identify this world-famous entertainer?

238. The marvelous trio of Bob Hope, Bing Crosby, and Dorothy Lamour made seven "Road" pictures in all. How many of these film titles can you name?

239. One of Hollywood's legendary stars made an abrupt change when he left behind roles as a crooner and became a dramatic actor and often "tough guy." Among his films were *Forty-Second Street; Hollywood Hotel; Murder, My Sweet;* and *Pitfall.* Among his three wives were actresses Joan Blondell and June Allyson. Who was this versatile performer?

240. A future famous actor was born in Johannesburg, South Africa in 1892. When sound came to films his voice made him a perfect villain, and he played articulate scoundrels in *David Copperfield, Captain Blood, Anna Karenina,* and *A Tale of Two Cities.* Then in 1939 20th Century Fox selected him to play a well-known character from literature. So successful was his performance that he played the famous character thirteen more times. In real life, he was considered to be Hollywood's best fencer, but as a villain he naturally had to lose. Only once did he "win" a duel on screen. Who was this splendid actor?

241. What is the most common nickname for players in the history of major league baseball?

236. Twelve. Remember, there's a face at both the top and bottom of the card.

237. Bing Crosby

238. *Road to Singapore* (1940), *Road to Zanzibar* (1941), *Road to Morocco* (1942), *Road to Utopia* (1945), *Road to Rio* (1947), *Road to Bali* (1952), *Road to Hong Kong* (1962)

239. Dick Powell

240. Basil Rathbone, famous for his portrayal of Sherlock Holmes

241. Lefty (Red is second and Doc third)

Army's "Mr. Inside" Felix "Doc" Blanchard (No. 35)
and "Mr. Outside" Glenn Davis (No. 41)

242. One of vintage radio's most delightful comedy programs featured Goodman Ace and his wife, Jane. She became well-known for her malapropisms such as "You've got to take the bitter with the batter," "I'm really in a quarry," "This hang-nail expression," and "Up at the crank of dawn." What was the name of the witty program?

243. A popular children's radio program began with the theme song "Who's that little chatterbox, the one with pretty auburn locks, who can it be..." Well, who was it?

244. Here's a football stumper. According to college rules, a player may not run or pass after his knee touches the ground while the ball is in his possession. But there is one exception. Which player may run or pass in such a case?

245. Only two common words in our language contain a double W, the letter W twice in a row. Can you think of one of them?

246. Muni Weisenfreund was born in Austria and became one of Hollywood's most celebrated stars. He won an Oscar for his performance in *The Story of Louis Pasteur* in 1936 and also starred in such notable films as *Scarface*, *I Am a Fugitive From a Chain Gang*, *The Life of Emile Zola*, and *The Good Earth*. By what name do we remember this distinguished performer?

247. If you add the letter A to the last name of a United States president, you have the name of a popular dance. What is the dance?

248. Louis is the most common name of French kings. There were eighteen of them. Philip is the most common among Spanish kings, with five. But what is the most common name for an English king?

242. "Easy Aces"

243. "Little Orphan Annie"

244. The placekick holder

245. *Glowworm* and *powwow* (you also get credit for *bow-wow*, which some dictionaries consider to be a word)

246. Paul Muni

247. Polka (President James K. Polk)

248. Edward (eleven of them: the eight numbered ones plus Edward the Elder, Edward the Martyr, and Edward the Confessor)

Little Orphan Annie shake-up mug

249. The popular radio show titled "Mr. District Attorney" that starred Jay Jostyn in the title role was inspired by the real-life racketbusting of a prominent D.A. He became governor of his state and was twice nominated for president. Who was he?

250. Here's an all-time favorite puzzle guaranteed to brighten up any dinner conversation or cocktail party. "Six men are each carrying six bags. Each bag contains six cats. Each cat has six kittens. How many legs are there altogether? (You're almost certain to have a variety of answers when you ask it of a group of people.)

251. A popular children's adventure series that began on network radio in 1932 was set originally on the "H-Bar-O Ranch" because it was sponsored by H-O Oats. When the sponsor left, the ranch became the "B-Bar-B Ranch." Can you identify the program?

252. One of Hollywood's legendary child actors started his career as a six-year-old member of *Our Gang,* the popular short subject also known as *The Little Rascals.* He was nominated for an Oscar for *Skippy* two years later and also starred in *The Champ* with Wallace Beery. He continued to act in movies as an adult and moved easily into television roles before becoming a TV executive. Who is he?

253. There are four widely played sports with eleven players on each team. How many can you name?

254. One of the top dance bands of the 1930s was led by a German-born trumpet player who had been a soloist for Paul Whiteman. In 1937 he had a number-one hit record of "With Plenty of Money and You." His theme song was "Hot Lips," and his first name was Henry. Can you identify him?

249. Thomas E. Dewey

250. 6,060 (6 men have 12 legs. 216 cats have 864 legs. 1,296 kittens have 5,184 legs. They add up to 6,060)

251. "Bobby Benson's Adventures"

252. Jackie Cooper

253. Football, soccer, cricket, and field hockey

254. Henry Busse

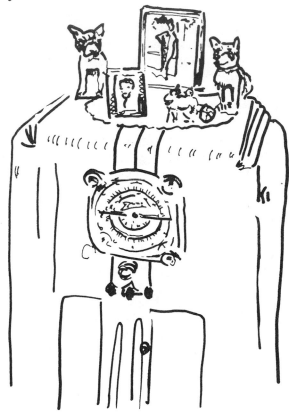

255. One of the many stars of *Gone With the Wind* won an Oscar that same year (1939) for a role in another film, *Stagecoach.* He made dozens of other films, but will always be best rememberd for his role as Scarlett O'Hara's father. His nephew James became secretary of labor under Eisenhower. Who was this splendid actor?

256. Two years before "Prince Valiant" appeared on the comic strip pages, another knight began entertaining readers. But he was drawn for laughs, and most of the strip's characters were rather zany. Eventually, the strip became a parody of the highly regarded "Prince Valiant," though in the satire no one ever seemed to get hurt seriously. Can you think of the name of this popular strip?

257. Here are the slogans of four well-known newspapers. Try to identify them.

a. "The Voice of the West"
b. "Covers Dixie Like the Dew"
c. "The World's Greatest Newspaper"
d. "All the News That's Fit to Print"

258. Only one heavyweight boxing champ had a brother who pitched in the major leagues. The champ, who reigned from 1892–1897, was portrayed on film by Errol Flynn. Who was that famous boxer?

259. Only one common word in the English language begins with the letters *rha.* What is the word?

260. Jason Robards, Senior, the father of the distinguished Jason Robards, Junior, played the title role in a popular radio program featuring a magician. It was not Mandrake or Blackstone. Who was the magician?

255. Thomas Mitchell

256. "Oaky Doaks," which ran from 1935–1961

257.
a. *San Francisco Chronicle*
b. *Atlanta Journal*
c. *Chicago Tribune*
d. *New York Times*

258. Jim Corbett (the film was *Gentleman Jim*). His brother, Joe, pitched in the National League for three different teams.

259. Rhapsody (or its derivatives such as rhapsodist and rhapsodic)

260. Chandu

Popeye's friend "The Jeep"

261. In the 1947 hit movie *The Egg and I*, Marjorie Main and Percy Kilbride had supporting roles as a hillbilly couple. Audiences loved them so much that in 1949 they began a series of seven films together featuring the couple. Can you recall the names of the characters they played?

262. We have a mystery athlete. He played centerfield for Notre Dame's baseball team in 1920 but did not achieve his dream of playing for the Chicago Cubs. He is remembered today as one of the most famous athletes in sports history—but for a different sport. Who was he?

263. In the 1940s a Southern politician wrote a popular song that he used in his successful campaign for governor. The state was Louisiana. The governor was Jimmie Davis. What was the song?

264. One of the 20th century's most versatile persons was a classical pianist who appeared in some movies and made many recordings. He also became prime minister of Poland. Who could that be?

265. In 1953 there were two hit songs that had lyrics completely in a foreign language. Julius LaRosa had one of the hits, actress Silvana Mangano the other. Can you name the two songs? LaRosa's went to number two on the charts and the other to number five.

266. A singer of the early 1950s named Carolyn Tempo was advised by her manager to change her name to "something more believable." She then proceeded to turn out some hit records in her intimate whispering vocal style. Best-remembered is "Gimme a Little Kiss, Will Ya, Huh?" Who was she?

267. What would you guess is the most common name for a person in the Bible? It's not John or Joseph or Mary...not Eli or Caleb or Saul. What can it be?

261. Ma and Pa Kettle

262. George Gipp, who led Notre Dame's football team in rushing and passing his last three seasons and was named by Walter Camp as the most outstanding college football player of 1920—the man we remember as The Gipper

263. "You Are My Sunshine"

264. Ignace Paderewski

265. "Eh Cumpari" (La Rosa) and "Anna" (Mangano)

266. April Stevens

267. Zechariah, the name of more than thirty people in the Bible

268. A popular comic strip that was subtitled "The Breadwinner" featured such characters as Perry, Will Wright, Spike, Spud, and Denny Dimwit. Can you name the strip?

269. An actor born as Frederick Bickel became one of America's most respected stage and screen stars. He won Academy Awards for *Dr. Jekyll and Mr. Hyde* and *The Best Years of Our Lives*. He was nominated for an Oscar for other films including *A Star Is Born* and *Death of a Salesman*. Can you name this distiguished actor?

270. One of the longest-running comic strips dealing with teenagers began in 1915 and featured such characters as Lard Smith, Hilda Grubble, and boy inventor Nutty Cook. The strip was named for an Andy Hardy-like boy and was called "_____ and His Friends." Can you fill in the missing name?

271. Only one boxer fought both Jack Dempsey and Joe Louis. He lost to Dempsey in 1927 by a TKO and lost to Louis in 1936 by a knockout. Both were nontitle bouts. But he finally won the heavyweight title in 1932 by defeating Max Schmeling. The following year he lost it to Primo Carnera. Who was it?

272. Here are two interesting words, each six letters long. One contains four *E*s, the other four *O*s. What are the words?

273. Only one entry in *Webster's Third Unabridged Dictionary* is capitalized. Do you know what the word is?

274. One of America's best-loved married couples started out in a band, he as the leader and she the featured vocalist. The band had a number-one hit in 1935, "And Then Some." Later they appeared together on Red Skelton's radio program and eventually had their own radio sitcom which moved into television in 1952. Who were these popular people?

268. "Winnie Winkle"

269. Fredric March

270. Freckles

271. Jack Sharkey

272. Teepee (tepee is an alternate spelling) and voodoo

273. God

274. Ozzie and Harriet (Ozzie Nelson and Harriet Hilliard)

275. Here's a list of six well-known people. Besides being bestselling authors, what did they have in common? A. J. Cronin, Peter Roget, Frank Slaughter, Benjamin Spock, Somerset Maugham, Arthur Conan Doyle

276. Many little girls have adorned the comic strip pages: Little Orphan Annie, Annie Rooney, Little Lulu, and so on. In the 1930s another little girl appeared occasionally in Jimmy Hatlo's "They'll Do it Every Time," and in 1943 was awarded her own strip. Who was this mischievous child?

277. There have been many famous sons of equally famous fathers in show business. Here are the first names of some well-known father-son combinations. Try to supply the last names.

a. Walter and John
b. Tex and John
c. Eddie and Peter
d. Douglas and Douglas

278. Here we go back to the old comic strips.

a. Perhaps you remember the one that often had the words "Notary Sojac" hanging in a picture frame. No one could figure out what the phrase meant. What was the strip?
b. Another strip featured a hitchhiker who stood by the side of the road saying "Nov Schmoz Ka Pop." What strip was that in?
c. Finally, what was the strip that featured a group of neighborhood kids who called themselves the Rinkydinks?

279. In the 1940s there were several prominent entertainers whose last name was Martin. You may remember Chris-Pin Martin, who provided comic relief in many western films. Tim Holt had a sidekick played by Richard Martin. See if you can recall four other famous show biz Martins of the 1940s, three singers and a bandleader.

275. They were all physicians. The best-selling writer in the group was Dr. Roget, who compiled *Roget's Thesaurus*.

276. Little Iodine (her last name was Tremblechin)

277.
a. Huston (Walter was a distinguished character actor of stage and screen. His son John became an outstanding film director as well as an actor and screenwriter. John was nominated for an Oscar in all three categories and won one for directing *The Treasure of Sierra Madre.* The film also brought his father an Oscar as best supporting actor.
b. Ritter (Tex sang the title song in the Gary Cooper film *High Noon.* His son John starred in TV's "Three's Company" series.)
c. Duchin (Both father and son were brilliant pianists and bandleaders.)
d. Fairbanks (Douglas Senior was one of the greatest stars of silent films in many acrobatic, swashbuckling roles. He was married to Mary Pickford. Douglas Junior was a durable screen actor with his peak years in the 1930s and 1940s.)

278.
a. "Smokey Stover"
b. "The Squirrel Cage"
c. "Winnie Winkle the Breadwinner"

279. Singers Tony Martin, Dean Martin, and Mary Martin; bandleader Freddy Martin

280. For six decades an actor named Emanuel Goldenberg lit up the silver screen. We know him by a different name, and we remember his performances in such films as *The Sea Wolf*, *Brother Orchid*, *Key Largo*, and *Double Indemnity*. He often played a gangster, but not always. Who was this dynamic actor?

281. A singer born as Clara Ann Fowler left her native Oklahoma with a new name and wound up with four number-one hits, "All My Love," "The Tennessee Waltz," "I Went to Your Wedding," and "The Doggie in the Window." Can you identify her?

282. One of old-time radio's best-remembered catch-phrases was spoken regularly by a supposedly ten-year-old Navajo boy adopted by a famous fictional cowboy. The program was a radio version of a popular comic strip by Fred Harman. What was the name of the boy, and what did he say repeatedly?

283. The first United States census was taken in the year 1790. What state would you guess was then the most populous?

284. A popular vocalist with Ted Weems's orchestra went on his own in 1942 and eventually had fourteen number-one hit songs. Among them were "Till the End of Time," "Surrender," "Prisoner of Love," "A You're Adorable," and "Hoop-Dee-Doo." Who was this singer from Canonsburg, Pennsylvania?

285. In the early 1930s, MGM signed a young medical student to act in films. He went on to become one of Hollywood's greatest stars, appearing in such films as *Magnificent Obsession*, *Bataan*, *Quo Vadis*, *Ivanhoe*, and *Billy the Kid*. Can you identify this handsome leading man?

280. Edward G. Robinson

281. Patti Page ("The Singing Rage")

282. Little Beaver, whose line was "You betchum, Red Ryder!"

283. Virginia, with a population then of 692,000. Pennsylvania was second and North Carolina third.

284. Perry Como

285. Robert Taylor

286. Out in America's heartland, near Chicago, a school chose "39ers" as its athletic team nickname. If you think carefully about it, you may be able to figure out what famous person they were honoring with the name selection.

287. Here's one for baseball fans. In 1948 a shortstop was chosen as the American League's Most Valuable Player. Twenty years later, in 1968, his son-in-law won the same award. Can you name the two players?

288. One of radio's most beloved characters was Pedro, played by Mel Blanc on a top-rated show hosted by a popular hillbilly singer turned comedienne. Pedro used to greet her with "Pardon me for talking in your face, señorita" in his Mexican accent. Other characters on the show included Geranium the maid, Aunt Aggie, and taxidriver Joe Crunchmiller. What was the program?

289. The consecutive letters *ressw* are found within a very common word, a word you often see in print or hear on the news. What is the word? (If you need a hint, think of Clare Boothe Luce.)

290. A popular program of a soap opera nature aired from 1932-1959 and tugged at the heartstrings of millions of listeners. Among the best remembered cast members were Paul, Hazel, Jack, Clifford, Nicky, Claudia, and the twins Hank and Pinky. Is that enough information to give you the answer to the name of the program?

291. Gertude Gearshift and Mabel Flapsaddle were telephone operators who used to make insulting comments about the host of the show. They were played by Sara Berner and Bea Benaderet. What was the program?

286. Jack Benny in his supposed hometown of Waukegan, Illinois. Jack, of course, always referred to himself as being 39 years old.

287. Lou Boudreau of Cleveland and pitcher Denny McLain of Detroit

288. "The Judy Canova Show"

289. Congresswoman

290. "One Man's Family," created by Carlton E. Morse

291. "The Jack Benny Program"

292. One of the greatest musical talents of the century was also an inventor who designed the first solid-body amplified electric guitar and developed sound-on-sound and multitrack recording techniques. With his wife as vocalist, he had two number-one hits, "How High the Moon" and "Vaya Con Dios." Can you name this incredible guitar player?

293. Many celebrities of the 1930s and 1940s had memorable first ames. Try to recall the last names of the following:

a. Tallulah
b. Hedda
c. Elisha
d. Darryl
e. Paulette
f. Claudette
g. Wendell
h. Louella
i. Cordell

294. The evil Moriarty was one of literature's most infamous villains as he battled Sherlock Holmes again and again. Here are some other fictional villains. See if you can recall the heroes they fought.

a. Dutch Cavendish
b. Killer Kane
c. Boris Arson
d. Ming the Merciless

295. In 1945 a Brooklyn Dodger utility player became the youngest player to ever hit a major league homerun. He was then 17 years old. Who was it?

296. A Swedish national risked his life to help many people escape the Nazis during World War II. He later died while a prisoner of the Soviets. The United States paid tribute to him by making him only the third person to become an honorary citizen, the other two being Lafayette and Churchill. Who was this heroic person?

292. Les Paul (his vocalist wife was Mary Ford)

293.
a. Bankhead
b. Hopper
c. Cook (Jr.)
d. Zanuck
e. Goddard
f. Colbert
g. Willkie (or Corey)
h. Parsons (middle initial O)
i. Hull

294.
a. The Lone Ranger
b. Buck Rogers
c. Dick Tracy
d. Flash Gordon

295. Tommy Brown

296. Raoul Wallenberg

297. Oldtime radio left us with many wonderful programs and a variety of catch-phrases some of us still recall. For example, Joe Penner's "Wanna buy a duck?" On what shows did we hear the following:

a. "Put something in the pot, boy!"
b. "Aren't we devils?"
c. "W-e-e-l-l-l, Daisy June!"
d. "It's a beautiful day in Chicago!"

298. A famous singing trio recorded six number-one songs: "Bei Mir Bist Du Schoen," "Ferryboat Serenade," "Shoo-Shoo Baby," "Rum and Coca-Cola," "I Can Dream, Can't I?" and "I Wanna Be Loved." Can you identify the trio?

299. What do military veterans refer to when they speak of a "Ruptured Duck"?

300. King Carol II abdicated his throne in 1940 rather than work with the Nazis and fled to Spain with his mistress Magda Lupescu. What was his native country?

301. A well-known fictional character of the comic strips was portrayed on film by such actors as Elmo Lincoln, Buster Crabbe, Herman Brix, Jock Mahoney, and Lex Barker. But the role is really "owned" by another actor who had been an Olympic athlete. Can you think of the character and the actor so closely associated with him?

302. Hannibal Cobb, Nick Charles, Philo Vance, Nero Wolfe, and Bulldog Drummond all shared the same occupation. What was it?

303. Two All-American football stars became cowboy movie stars. One was a halfback for Alabama and played in the Rose Bowl. The other was a bruising fullback from Texas A&M. Who were they?

297.
a. Jack Kirkwood on the "Bob Hope Pepsodent Show"
b. Ralph Edwards, the M.C. on "Truth or Consequences," said it often to the audience as he sent contestants out on some embarrassing or difficult mission
c. "The Red Skelton Show"
d. M.C. Everett Mitchell opened up each broadcast of "The National Farm and Home Hour" with that line, regardless of what the weather actually was. If it was foul weather he would add that fact but would then insist it was stilll a beautiful day.

298. The Andrews Sisters (Patty, Maxene, and LaVerne)

299. A lapel pin awarded to armed forces veterans for honorable service between September 8, 1938, and December 31, 1946. "Ruptured Duck" was also the name of the B-25 piloted by Captain Ted Lawson in the Doolittle raid on Tokyo in 1942.

300. Romania

301. Tarzan, played by Johnny Weissmuller

302. Detective

303. Johnny Mack Brown and "Jarrin' John" Kimbrough

304. A comedian nicknamed "Banjo-eyes" used to talk about his five daughters Natalie, Edna, Marilyn, Janet, and Marjorie, as well as his wife, Ida. Who was he?

305. A Hollywood character actor gained fame wth his squeaky voice that resulted from falling as a child with a stick in his mouth. He also appeared regularly for a long time on the Jack Benny radio program, greeting the star with "Hiya, Buck!" Who was he?

306. The signature song of one of the silver screen's most popular baritones was "Short'nin' Bread." Can you identify him?

307. "America's Boyfriend" eventually married "America's Sweetheart." Who were they?

308. Between 1915 and 1944 Edmund Gibson starred in some 200 silent films and 75 talkies as a cowboy hero. But he was better known by his nickname than as Edmund. What was his nickname?

309. Hollywood has had many performers with siblings who also starred on the silver screen. See if you can name the brothers of the following:

a. Tom Conway
b. Steve Forrest
c. Peter Graves
d. Arthur Shields
e. The sister of Olivia de Havilland

310. One of moviedom's legendary actors did not appear in a Hollywood film until he was 62 years old, but then made 24 of them, including *Casablanca* and *The Maltese Falcon*, for which he won an Academy Award nomination. Who was this 280-pound star?

304. Eddie Cantor

305. Andy Devine

306. Nelson Eddy

307. Buddy Rogers and Mary Pickford

308. "Hoot"

309.
a. George Sanders
b. Dana Andrews
c. James Arness
d. Barry Fitzgerald
e. Joan Fontaine

310. Sydney Greenstreet

311. Many of Hollywood's greatest stars were born in foreign countries. Try to name the land of birth of the following:

a. Sonja Henie
b. Carmen Miranda
c. Maurice Chevalier
d. Marlene Dietrich
e. Charlie Chaplin
f. Errol Flynn
g. Warner Oland

312. Many people remember that Batman's name was actually Bruce Wayne and Superman was Clark Kent. But who can recall the real identity of the following:

a. The Shadow
b. The Saint
c. The Falcon
d. The Green Hornet
e. Captain Marvel

313. Can you identify the creators of the following fictional heroes?

a. Perry Mason
b. Sam Spade
c. Nero Wolfe
d. Ellery Queen
e. Charlie Chan
f. Philo Vance

314. Political bosses have played a major role in urban development in the United States, including such leaders as "Big Bill" Thompson and Richard Daley in Chicago and William Tweed and Carmine DeSapio in New York. One of the most iron-fisted of all was the man who controlled Memphis, Tennessee for decades. His nickname was simply "Boss." Who was he?

311.

a. Norway

b. Portugal (she moved to Brazil as a baby)

c. France

d. Germany

e. England

f. Tasmania

g. Sweden

312.

a. Lamont Cranston

b. Simon Templar

c. Michael Waring

d. Britt Reid

e. Billy Batson

313.

a. Erle Stanley Gardner

b. Dashiell Hammett

c. Rex Stout

d. Frederic Dannay and Manfred Bennington Lee

e. Earl Derr Biggers

f. S. S.Van Dine

314. Edward H. Crump

315. A once popular comic strip featured such characters as Eugene the Jeep, The Sea-Hag, Roughhouse, Ham Gravy, and George W. Geezil. Can you identify the strip?

316. A famous comedian played such fictional characters on screen as Rufus T. Firefly, Professor Wagstaff, Dr. Hackenbush, Wolf J. Flywheel, S. Quentin Quale, Mr. Hammer, Otis B. Driftwood, and J. Cheever Loophole. Who was he?

317. Jim Backus appeared on a radio series as "Hubert Updike," a pompous, wealthy character who once sold his "Cah-dillac" because it was parked in the wrong direction. On what program was he a regular?

318. In the 1930s a famous radio comedienne got the nation's attention by embarking on a search for her supposedly missing brother. She would barge into network broadcasts trying to find him, although in real life her brother was at home leading a normal life. Who was she?

319. One of the nation's best-loved quiz programs began the broadcast with a rooster crowing and the words "Wake up, America. It's time to stump the experts." What was the name of this erudite panel show moderated by Clifton Fadiman?

320. Jack, Reggie, and Doc appeared each week in a radio adventure series that many critics considered the greatest program on the airwaves. It was created by the man who gave us "One Man's Family," Carlton E. Morse. What was the title of the adventure series?

321. For two decades a Saturday night radio show gave us country music and humor and featured a group whose segment began with "Are you ready, Hezzie?" Try to name the group and the program.

315. "Thimble Theatre Starring Popeye"

316. Groucho Marx (the films were respectively *Duck Soup, Horse Feathers, A Day at the Races, The Big Store, Go West, Cocoanuts, A Night at the Opera,* and *At the Circus*)

317. "The Alan Young Show"

318. Gracie Allen

319. "Information, Please!"

320. "I Love a Mystery"

321. The Hoosier Hot Shots, who used bulb horns, washboards, and a slide whistle for their lively music on "The National Barn Dance."

Edward Bowes on "Major Bowes
and His Original Amateur Hour"

322. Often overlooked when recalling the great female pop singers of the 1950s is a recording artist who sang solo on two number-one hits and three others that reached the number-two spot on the charts. Eight more she recorded made the top ten. It was not Rosemary Clooney, Ella Fitzgerald, Sarah Vaughan, Dinah Shore, Dinah Washington, Doris Day, Keely Smith, Patti Page, Helen O'Connell, Georgia Gibbs, Jo Stafford, Joni James, Peggy Lee, Kitty Kallen, Kay Starr, or Margaret Whiting. Who can it be? (If you'd like a hint, the number-one songs were "How High the Moon" and "Vaya Con Dios.")

323. Tiny Tim and Invisible Scarlet O'Neil were featured in comic strips in which each had an incredible power. What was it that they could do?

324. During Hollywood's Golden Years four stars with the last name of Powell lit up the screen. They were not related. Can you name all four (two men and two women)?

325. During World War Two, General Frank Merrill trained the 5307th Composite Group in guerrilla warfare and led them into battle as the first American infantrymen to fight in Asia. Can you recall the nickname given to his men?

326. The man considered by historians to be the first resistance leader in Europe against the Nazis in occupied territory led his forces in his native Yugoslavia but later battled fellow countryman Josip Broz Tito. Althought the noted freedom fighter's son and daughter both fought with Tito during the war, he was executed by a firing squad in 1946 on charges of treason. Who was this well-known soldier?

327. Italian Foreign Minister Count Ciano had a famous father-in-law. Unfortunately for the Count, his father-in-law had him executed by firing squad in 1944. Who was his father-in-law?

322. Mary Ford, who sang with her guitarist husband Les Paul on so many hits for Capitol Records.

323. Tiny Tim first appeared in 1931 as a Lilliputian-sized boy in a full-sized world. Twelve years later creator Stanley Link enabled him to change at will from his two-inch height to normal size and then back again. The strip appeared only on Sundays. Scarlet O'Neil, who came along in 1940 on a daily basis, could make herself visible or invisible by simply pressing a nerve on her left wrist. Creator Russell Stamm made it possible after she accidentally walked in front of a ray device invented by her scientist father.

324. Dick Powell, Eleanor Powell, Jane Powell, and William Powell.

325. "Merrill's Marauders"

326. Draza Mihajlovic

327. Italian dictator Benito Mussolini

328. Pete Gray, an outfielder with the St. Lous Browns in 1945, and Boid Buie, who gave shooting exhibitions from mid-court at halftime for the Harlem Globetrotters in the 1940s, had something most unusual in common. What was their common link?

329. Two of the best-known newspaper columns of the 1940s were titled "The Conning Tower" and "My Day." Can you recall the two famous people who wrote them?

330. Beginning a tempestuous political career as campaign manager of Fiorello H. LaGuardia's bid for re-election to Congress, a radical politician was himself elected to Congress in 1934 as a Republican. He was unabashedly pro-Communist, though he never joined the U.S. Communist Party. In 1950 he was the only member of Congress to vote against President Truman's ordering of U.S. troops into Korea. When he died, the Roman Catholic archdiocese refused to permit his burial in consecrated ground. Who was this controversial political leader?

331. In 1939 a famous American contralto was denied the use of Constitution Hall in Washington, D.C., for a concert. The Daughters of the American Revolution barred her because she was black. Eleanor Roosevelt then resigned from the DAR and got the U.S. government to allow this singer to hold her concert at the Lincoln Memorial. A live audience of 75,000 attended, and millions more heard the Easter morning concert on the radio. Who was the singer?

328. Each had only one arm

329. Franklin P. Adams and Eleanor Roosevelt

330. Vito Marcantonio

331. Marian Anderson

V-J Day celebration in New York's Times Square (August, 1945)

332. How well do you know your Captains? If you were asked to name a Captain who entertained America's youngsters on television. . .played by Bob Keeshan. . .you would say Captain Kangaroo. Let's see if you can identify these other Captains.

a. A caped hero of the comic books and movie serials who disappeared after the creators of Superman claimed copyright infringement. He could change from a crippled newspaper boy to a mighty hero by simply saying "Shazam," which stood for the initials of Solomon, Hercules, Atlas, Zeus, Achilles, and Mercury.

b. An early television space hero seen on Dumont as early as 1949, played first by Richard Coogan, then by Al Hodge.

c. The superpatriot who battled our nation's enemies clad in a spectacular red, white, and blue costume. He originated in comic books in 1941 and later appeared in a Republic Studios movie serial.

d. An aviator of radio, television, and movie serials who headed The Secret Squadron and was aided by squadron members Ikky Mudd, Chuck Ramsey, and Joyce Ryan.

333. The name Koken has been stared at by generations of American men and boys and even many women as well. Where does that name appear?

334. Only three men ever knocked down Joe Louis while he was heavyweight boxing champion of the world. How many can you name?

332.
a. Captain Marvel
b. Captain Video
c. Captain America
d. Captain Midnight

333. It's in the footrest of a barber chair. The name Koken is embodied in the metal step.

334. Two-ton Tony Galento, Buddy Baer, and Jersey Joe Walcott

Jean Harlow "The Platinum Blonde" (1911-1937)

335. Here are some characters from old-time radio shows. Try to identify the program.

a. Deadeye, Clem Kadiddlehopper, Daisy June, and The Mean Widdle Kid.
b. Mayor LaTrivia, Wallace Wimple, Sis, and Doc Gamble
c. Judge Hooker, Birdie the maid, Peavey the druggist, and Leroy the nephew

336. One of the most famous of all old-time radio programs featured a comical pair who earlier on radio billed themselves as The Smackouts. Who were they?

337. A famous Marine Corps pilot of World War II was awarded the Congressional Medal of Honor and later became governor of South Dakota. Can you recall his name?

338. Two well-known athletes of the past both had the first name "Dolph." One was a pro basketball star; the other was a major league first baseman. Who were they?

339. In 1948 a popular female vocalist went to the top of the charts with her Capitol recording of "A Tree in the Meadow." She grew up in California surrounded by famous songwriters such as Johnny Mercer and Jerome Kern, for her father was himself an accomplished composer, writing or co-writing such songs as "Sleepy Time Gal," "The Japanese Sandman," "Till We Meet Again," "Ain't We Got Fun?", "My Ideal," "On the Good Ship Lollipop," "Too Marvelous for Words," "Beyond the Blue Horizon," and "You're An Old Smoothie." Who was the singer?

340. Three notorious criminals of a bygone era took pride in their nicknames: Pretty Boy, Scarface, and Machinegun. Can you identify them?

335.
a. Red Skelton
b. Fibber McGee and Molly
c. The Great Gildersleeve

336. Fibber McGee and Molly. In the role of the Smackouts, Jim Jordan was a grocer who was always "smackout" of nearly everything.

337. Joe Foss

338. Dolph Schayes and Dolph Camilli

339. Margaret Whiting, whose father was Richard Whiting

340. Pretty Boy Floyd, Al Capone, and Machinegun Kelly

341. The first popular patriotic song in the United States after Pearl Harbor became the number-eight tune only seven weeks after the attack. It was titled, appropriately, "Remember Pearl Harbor" (it began, "Let's remember Pearl Harbor as we go to meet the foe") and was co-written and recorded by one of America's top bandleaders. Who was he?

342. One of the best-known women in the United States during World War II was an army colonel who headed the WACs (Women's Army Corps). In 1953 she took office in the Eisenhower administration as the first secretary of Health, Education, and Welfare. Who was she?

343. Cartoonist Bill Mauldin depicted two grizzled GIs in his newspaper series "Up Front." What were the names of these hapless soldiers often depicted with bullets whizzing overhead?

344. A Pulitzer Prize-winning war correspondent who had covered the London Blitz and combat in North Africa, Sicily, France, and the Pacific while reporting on the "average" GI was killed by machinegun fire on Ie Shima, an island off northwestern Okinawa in 1945. Who was this beloved journalist?

345. In the 1930s and well into the 1940s, nearly every house in the United States had a card about a foot square in a front window with the numbers 25, 50, 75, and 100 on it. The numbers were arranged on the card so that only one of them was right side up as viewed from the street. What was the purpose of this almost universally used system?

341. Sammy Kaye (his co-writer was Don Reid)

342. Oveta Culp Hobby

343. Willie and Joe

344. Ernie Pyle

345. The card was placed in the window to indicate to the iceman whether to deliver a 25, 50, 75, or 100 pound block of ice.

Louis Armstrong

346. One of the most amazing things about vintage radio is the tremendous sponsor identification many of the programs enjoyed—and still do to this day, in some cases more than sixty years later. For example, Oxydol's own Ma Perkins. See if you can name the longtime sponsors of the following shows:

a. "Jack Armstrong, the All-American Boy"
b. "Tom Mix"
c. "Your Hit Parade"
d. "Fibber McGee and Molly"

347. Try to identify the following performers from their nicknames.

a. The It Girl
b. The Sweater Girl
c. The Oomph Girl
d. The Platinum Blonde
e. The Blonde Bombshell

348. Blondie and Dagwood are well-known comic strip characters whose names go together like ham and eggs. Let's return to some old-time strips and see if you can name the characters that complement the following:

a. Hans and _____
b. Mutt and _____
c. Jiggs and _____
d. Alphonse and _____
e. Abbie an' _____

349. "From here to Timbuktu" was once a very common expression. Yet many people who used it had no idea in what country Timbuktu is located. Do you know?

346.
a. Wheaties
b. Ralston cereal ("Tom Mix and the Ralston Straight-Shooters are on the air!")
c. Lucky Strike
d. Johnson's Wax, which sponsored the show for eighteen years beginning in 1935

347.
a. Clara Bow
b. Lana Turner
c. Ann Sheridan
d. Jean Harlow
e. Betty Hutton

348.
a. Hans and Fritz, the Katzenjammer Kids (the word in German refers to a howling of cats, in other words, a hangover)
b. Mutt and Jeff, who have been around since 1907
c. Jiggs and Maggie, the unhappily married couple of "Bringing Up Father"
d. Alphonse and Gaston. The strip was created in 1902 by Frederick Opper, who earlier had great success with Happy Hooligan. Alphonse and Gaston dressed in 19th-century clothes and never lost their good manners even in the face of catastrophe. They were constantly bowing and scraping and saying, "After you, my dear Alphonse." "No, after you, my dear Gaston."
e. Abbie an' Slats, a popular strip from 1937 to 1971. It was a collaboration of Al Capp and Raeburn Van Buren. Capp, of Li'l Abner fame, handled the story part, while Van Buren drew it. Bathless Groggins was one of the most memorable characters in "Abbie an' Slats."

349. The exotic city of Timbuktu is in the African nation of Mali, which until 1958 was known as French Sudan.

350. In the 1940s the name Robert graced the marquee of many movie theaters with ten leading men by that name. How many leading men of the 1940s whose first name was Robert can you think of?

351. This puzzle is certainly no bed of roses, for it is one of the most difficult in this book. Rare is the person who can solve it. Here's a big hint: It helps if you are a sports fan. What do the following nine words have in common? Decidedly, Worth, Determine, Pensive, Affirmed, Cavalcade, Regret, Ponder, Plaudit

352. See if you can recall the civilian post held during World War II by the following:

a. Cordell Hull
b. Henry L. Stimson
c. Frank Knox

353. A U.S. Navy Lieutenant shot down five Japanese aircraft in one day (February 20, 1942) to become the Navy's first ace ever. A huge airport was named for him. What's his name?

354. Through the years the marriages of Hollywood movie stars have often received as much attention as the roles they have played on screen. See if you can identify the movie stars who had multiple marriages to the following:

a. An actress married to William Powell and Clark Gable
b. An actor married to Joan Blondell and June Allyson
c. An actress married to Jackie Coogan and bandleader Harry James
d. An actress married to Mickey Rooney, Frank Sinatra, and bandleader Artie Shaw
e. An actor married to Zsa Zsa Gabor, Magda Gabor, and Benita Hume (the widow of Ronald Colman)

350. Robert Alda, Robert Cummings, Robert Donat, Robert Mitchum, Robert Montgomery, Robert Preston, Robert Stack, Robert Taylor, Robert Walker, and Robert Young.

351. They were all winners of the Kentucky Derby. It would have been easier had we included Citation, Swaps, Omaha, and Whirlaway, but who wants easy?

352.
a. Secretary of State
b. Secretary of War
c. Secretary of the Navy

353. Edward H. O'Hare (Chicago's O'Hare Airport)

354.
a. Carole Lombard
b. Dick Powell
c. Betty Grable
d. Ava Gardner
e. George Sanders

355. Let's test your knowledge of college football history. Grantland Rice wrote about The Four Horsemen of Notre Dame: quarterback Harry Stuhldreher, halfbacks Sleepy Jim Crowley and Don Miller, and fullback Elmer Layden. The Four Horsemen played thirty games in all, losing only two. Both losses were to the same university. What team won those two games?

356. Born Helen Gould Beck in 1904, this woman left behind a career in silent movies to appear as Lady Godiva at the 1933 Chicago World's Fair. Dancing with two seven-foot ostrich feather fans (and nothing else), she attracted huge crowds and became world-famous. What was the provocative dancer's show-business name?

357. From 1919 to 1953 a former Wanamaker Department Store clerk served as New York City's official greeter. He instituted the city's renowned ticker-tape parades, served for 18 months as New York City police commissioner from 1928 to 1930, and proposed the 1939–1940 New York World's Fair. Who was he?

358. Here are some once well-known names from old-time radio. Try to recall on which program they appeared regularly. Joel Kupperman, Ruth Duskin, Harve Fischman, Cynthia Cline, Patrick Conlon, Geraldine Hamburg, Van Dyke Tiers, Gerard Darrow, and Joan Bishop.

359. Let's recall some familiar theme songs of the 1930s and 1940s.

a. A radio soap opera that used as its theme song "Red River Valley"
b. A popular radio program featuring as its theme "When Irish Eyes Are Smiling"
c. A musical program using "Lucky Day" as its theme.

355. Nebraska

356. Sally Rand

357. Grover Whalen

358. The Quiz Kids. The very first question asked by M.C. Joe Kelly on June 28, 1940, was "I want you to tell me what I would be carrying home if I brought an antimacassar, a dinghy, a sarong, and an apteryx." (In case you don't know, an antimacassar is a cover to protect the back or arms of furniture from Macassar oil or other hair preparations. A dinghy is a small boat. A sarong is a loose cloth skirt worn by men and women in the Malay archipelago and some Pacific islands. An apteryx is a flightless bird such as the kiwi.)

359.
a. "Our Gal Sunday" ("The story asks the question. . .can this girl from a mining town in the West find happiness as the wife of a wealthy and titled Englishman?").
b. No, it's not "Abie's Irish Rose. That show used "My Wild Irish Rose" as its theme. "When Irish Eyes Are Smiling" introduced "Duffy's Tavern" ("Hello, Duffy's Tavern, where the elite meet to eat. Archie the manager speaking. Duffy ain't here. . .oh, hello, Duffy.")
c. "Your Hit Parade" ("as determined by 'Your Hit Parade' survey, which checks the best-sellers in sheet music and phonograph records, the songs most heard on the air and most played in the automatic coin machines—an accurate, authentic tabulation of America's taste in popular music."

360. When Jesse Owens won the 200-meter dash in the 1936 Olympics in Berlin, second place went to the older brother of a man who became one of the most famous athletes in the history of sports. What was the name of that younger brother?

361. "The Colgate Sports Newsreel" was one of radio's most popular broadcasts during its network run from September 1939 to June 1951. The theme was sung in barbershop-quartet style to the tune of "Mademoiselle from Armentières" and the sportscaster who hosted the broadcast always signed off with "And that's our three-o mark for tonight!" Who was the sportscaster?

360. Jackie Robinson, whose older brother Mack Robinson came in second to Jesse Owens

361. Bill Stern

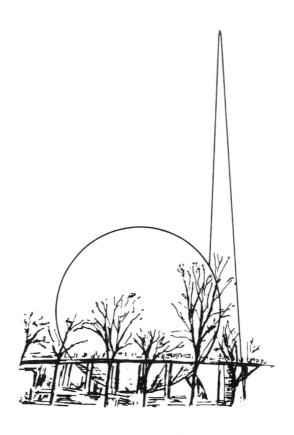

The Perisphere and Trylon of the 1939 New York World's Fair

About the Author

Bill Owen, whose career is highlighted in Jim Lowe's "Foreword," first earned his reputation for interesting trivia as the announcer on ABC-TV's "World News This Morning" from 1982–1990. There he attracted a massive cult-like following for his brief comments leading into commercial breaks. Audiences were fascinated with his puzzles, quotations, and odd facts to the extent that the show's producers acknowledged that people tuned in more for Bill's bits than the news itself. At the time, viewers demanded, even begged, that he make a book out of them. Here, at last, is his response.

About the Illustrator

Carolyn Owen, the daughter of author Bill Owen, is not only a talented artist with a wide range of styles but an accomplished musician as well. Carolyn was born in Bismarck, North Dakota, and has lived in California, Oregon, Ohio, and New York and was educated at colleges in San Diego, New York City, and Evian, France. She composes and performs her own music and has been highly praised by audiences and critics alike for her creativity. Carolyn is an enthusiastic skier and hiker, loves to ride horses, and lives near Ithaca, New York, with her many pet animals.